Three Minutes a Day

VOLUME 41

Other Christopher Books in Print

Father James Keller's
You Can Change the World
Anniversary Edition

and other volumes in the

Three Minutes a Day
series

THREE MINUTES A DAY
VOLUME 41

Dennis Heaney
President, The Christophers

Stephanie Raha
Editor-in-Chief

Margaret O'Connell
Senior Research Editor

Staff Contributing Editors
Lisa Mantineo
Nicholas Monteleone
Anna Marie Tripodi

Contributors
Joan Bromfield
Monica Ann Yehle-Glick
Karen Hazel Radenbaugh

Contributing Interns
Mike Arthur
Dunja Dunda
Maria Giura
Qwenchia Kimbrough
Jaclynn Szczepaniec
Keri Tan

The Christophers
12 East 48th Street
New York, NY 10017

Let love be genuine; hate what is evil, hold fast to what is good; love one another with mutual affection; outdo one another in showing honor. Do not lag in zeal, be ardent in spirit, serve the Lord. Rejoice in hope, be patient in suffering, persevere in prayer. Contribute to the needs of the saints; extend hospitality to strangers.

Bless those who persecute you; bless and do not curse them. Rejoice with those who rejoice, weep with those who weep. Live in harmony with one another.

ROMANS 12:9-16

Introduction

This is a happy year for The Christophers. We are celebrating not only the release of this book, volume 41 in our *Three Minutes a Day* series, but also the publication of *Father James Keller's You Can Change the World Anniversary Edition*. Both books challenge you, the reader, to be a Christopher, or Christbearer.

Father Keller had a vision—"The Christopher gets out of his own little world and into the big world. ...You will be fulfilling the purpose for which you were created: to love God above all things and your neighbor as yourself."

Edited by Gerald M. Costello, a Christopher board member and award-winning journalist, the new *You Can Change the World* edition encourages you to use your God-given talents and abilities to take positive action.

And *Three Minutes a Day* aims to inspire you to accomplish your unique mission. Taking a few minutes a day for reflection and prayer adds perspective, as you realize the power and possibilities in your own life.

Our prayer is that Christopher literature encourages you to light many candles of hope.

Peace!

Dennis Heaney
President, The Christophers

Scheduling the Year on New Year's Day

Every year, Jenny Collins-Friedrichs takes a look at her life on New Year's Day—and gets started on her year's "to do" list.

On January 1, 2005, with thoughts of adoption running through her mind, this Seattle mother of two children was scanning the Web when she found information about an agency that has placed thousands of foreign-born orphans with American families. She and her husband Brian started reading through the stories of children from Addis Ababa, Ethiopia, when the profile of one eight-year-old girl, Meseret, caught their attention.

"Both her parents were dead, and her brother and sister had been separated from her," she says. "Here was a soul and a spirit that needed to be nourished. We knew it would be a privilege to have that soul flourish within our family."

When there's a task to be done or a goal to be reached, there's no time like "right now" to get started.

Religion...is this: to care for orphans and widows in their distress, and to keep oneself unstained by the world. (James 1:27)

Remind us, Lord, to do the best we can with each moment of each day You give us.

What's the Good Word?

When you see someone who seems sad or discouraged do you say a good word? Your encouragement may be exactly what that person needs.

That's why, while waiting at an airport, professional speaker Jim Cathcart made an effort to help a young man. Cathcart was at a crowded food court when he noticed a busboy clearing away dishes and trash from the tables. His shoulders were slumped; he kept his head down and barely looked at anyone.

Wanting to do something for the busboy, Cathcart said, "If you weren't doing what you are doing, it wouldn't be five minutes before there was trash everywhere, and people would stop coming here. What you are doing is important, and I just wanted to say thanks for doing it." The busboy smiled. He stood taller and started making eye contact with people.

Encourage those who could benefit from a kind word–and that's just about everyone.

Encourage one another. (1 Thessalonians 4:18)

Inspire my words to reflect Your love for each of us, Father of all.

Getting (Y-a-w-n) Sleepy?

If you find yourself dozing off at your desk, or snoozing on the sofa long before bedtime, it may be time to re-examine your health habits.

For example, simply not hydrating your body sufficiently can zap your energy. Drink water throughout the day, every day, and you might see your energy level improve.

Another way to help boost energy is to make sure you not only get enough rest, but that you get the right kind of rest. If you don't maintain a somewhat consistent pattern of going to bed at about the same time each night for roughly eight hours, you could be robbing your body of much needed rest.

Vitamins could also put some vim back in your vigor. Ask your doctor which ones might be right for you.

Sometimes, the most nagging problems can be solved with relatively simple solutions.

God of my ancestors and Lord of mercy...give me the wisdom that sits by Your throne, and do not reject me from among Your servants. (Wisdom of Solomon 9:1,4)

Give me mental clarity, Spirit of Truth, so that I may better respond to life's challenges.

A Letter-Perfect Friendship

They started as 14-year-olds writing each other across an ocean as World War II came to an end. They ended up as life-long pals.

And although they've never met, after 61 years of sharing each other's pains and joys; shedding tears over tragic losses and happy weddings, Gloria Lipset of Brooklyn, New York, and Margaret Stainthorpe of Northumberland, England, feel the bond of a shared lifetime.

Now, although they've talked on the telephone, the two have no plans to meet. "We'll continue sharing our lives through our letters," offers Stainthorpe. "We've helped each other that way all these years."

Knowing that someone is on our side, loving us and wishing us well, makes all the difference in the world.

The eyes of the Lord are on those who love Him, a mighty shield and strong support, a shelter from scorching wind and a shade from noonday sun, a guard against stumbling and a help against falling. (Sirach 34:19)

Help me lend my support to someone today, Merciful Trinity.

Beyond the Sounds of Silence

As a child, did you ever make a telephone with a string and two cans or paper cups? Do you know how it worked?

If you keep the string straight and taut while one person speaks and the other listens, words cause the bottom of the cup to vibrate with sound waves. These vibrations (1,000 times or more per second) travel through the string making the bottom of the second cup vibrate, too. The listener hears the sound waves.

That's basically how a real telephone works, but with electric current replacing string. It seems simple, but it took the discovery of nature's laws by scientists coupled with their creativity for us to be able to say "Hello!" across the miles.

Alexander Graham Bell is credited with inventing the telephone, yet there were and are many other talented and innovative men and women. Let's reflect on the thanks we owe those who make our lives easier.

**I have given skill to all the skillful.
(Exodus 31:6)**

We praise You, Holy Creator, for the intelligence, curiosity and determination with which You've blessed Your people.

Teenagers on the Air

Six years ago, freelance radio producer Marianne McCune started *Radio Rookies*. "The idea," she said, "was to teach teens to introduce themselves to the public in a way people can listen to and not just turn off because they're wearing the wrong clothes or talking the wrong way." Aired on WNYC-FM in New York, a National Public Radio affiliate, the programs tackle a wide variety of subject matter–graffiti, wayward siblings, birth, death, racism, virginity, disability, fashion, obsession, aggression, parents.

"These pieces cross the line between journalism and personal narrative," says WNYC vice-president of programming, Dean Cappello. "This is a way of putting voices on the air that will speak to kids in the listening audience, and give other listeners a glimpse into people they might never otherwise have a relationship with."

Young or old, each of us needs to be heard. Have you listened to someone today?

Teach me, O Lord, the way of your statutes... Give me understanding, that I may keep Your law...with my whole heart. (Psalm 119:33,34)

I am listening for Your voice, Lord. Whisper love to me. Guide me in the way everlasting.

Chalk It Up to Tradition

Every holiday and holy day has its own traditions–some better known than others.

Peter Gilmour, who teaches at the Institute of Pastoral Studies of Loyola University Chicago, tells how his church celebrates the feast of the Epiphany. Pieces of chalk are blessed by the priest with the words, "May God, who provided a safe dwelling for the eternal Word, bless this chalk, the homes of the faithful, and the people who live there, through Christ our Lord. Amen."

Families take a piece home to write an inscription above the door: "20+C+M+B+07." The numbers refer to the year and the letters to the initials of the names customarily given to the Three Wise Men–Caspar, Melchior and Balthasar. It's a way of connecting our own homes with the first home of the Infant Jesus.

Traditions connect us with the past, with our faith and with one another. Celebrate them with your loved ones.

After eight days had passed, it was time to circumcise the Child; and He was called Jesus, the name given by the angel before He was conceived in the womb. (Luke 2:21)

Infant Jesus, may we welcome You into our homes and our hearts with joy and gladness.

Words...Wonderful Words

Question: where did the American English words savvy, ranch, alligator, cafeteria, cargo, cigar or cigarette, guerrilla, mosquito, barracuda, vanilla, tornado, tuna and comrade originate?

It's estimated that the Spanish language has contributed 10,000 words to English through the rich Mexican culture of the southwest.

The Nahuatl, Quechua (Inca), Arawak, Carib, Guarani and Taino Indians of the Caribbean and South America contributed tomato (tomatl), chocolate (xocolatl), potato (papa), jaguar (yaguar) and iguana (iwana).

Imagine, if you can, how dull it would be without such linguistic diversity. Study the origins of words so as to appreciate the great gift of language which God granted us.

In the beginning was the Word, and the Word was with God, and the Word was God. (John 1:1)

Imbue us with a deep respect—and delight—in the cultural and linguistic diversity of this land, Word of God.

The Importance of Remorse

Ryan Cushing and four other teens bought a 20-pound frozen turkey with a stolen credit card. Cushing hurled the frozen bird out the side window of a speeding car. The missile smashed through Victoria Ruvolo's car windshield, broke every bone in her face and knocked her unconscious. Had her passenger not managed to steer the car off the road, they would have crashed.

Cushing could have received up to 25 years in prison on multiple felony charges. Instead, he gave Ruvolo a handwritten four-page apology. And, uncoached, he wept in her arms, remorsefully.

While not condoning the teen's behavior, Victoria Ruvolo said, "God gave me a second chance at life, and I passed it on." Ryan Cushing was sentenced to six months in jail and five years' probation.

Disarm those who have hurt you in any way with mercy. Give them a chance to take responsibility for the consequences of their actions.

Blessed are the merciful, for they will receive mercy. (Matthew 5:7)

Jesus, remind me that, as Shakespeare wrote, "...mercy...blesseth those that give and those that receive (it)." Help me to be merciful.

Trading in a Home to Make a House

In 1993, Linda and Gary Tatu lost everything–deliberately.

They sold their large Amherst, New York, house, where they entertained with parties for more than 100 people, and gave up extravagant "toys" like a 28-foot cabin cruiser to purchase a dilapidated church in Buffalo.

After living an entire year without heat during renovations, the couple transformed the church into Harvest House which provides meeting space for community organizations, Bible study groups, and spiritual retreats.

Harvest House is also home to outreach programs, among them Baby and Children's Outreach which helps thousands of babies and children each year. In fact, today it's the largest supplier in the area of free baby items, as well as baby and children's clothing.

The Tatus learned to value what really matters. We all need to do that, too.

I prayed, and understanding was given to me; the spirit of wisdom came to me.
(Wisdom of Solomon 7:7)

Redeemer, teach us to value human beings and all Creation, the works of Your hands, more than things.

High Achievement

This is the story of a youngster, diagnosed with autism, who defied expectations. It's also a story of teamwork and community support.

Although passionate about basketball, Jason McElwain, 17, of Rochester, New York, never made his high school teams. But he became student manager and rarely missed practice. The point guard says, "He's so much fun to be around. He's got a lot of enthusiasm."

Possibly out of kindness, the coach put Jason in during the final minutes of the "Senior Night" game, traditionally a time when graduating seniors who never played or scored much get a last chance.

Surprisingly, Jason started making baskets. The fans cheered in support. Teammates who would have themselves liked to score instead kept passing him the ball. He made 20 points.

Don't underestimate people with learning or emotional handicaps. Encourage them; remember that no one makes it alone in life; and shoot for the stars yourself.

Convince, rebuke and encourage with the utmost patience in teaching. (2 Timothy 4:2)

Help us not to underestimate our own or others' abilities, Jesus.

Hard-Won Wisdom

People newly diagnosed with a serious illness benefit from the expert opinions of doctors. But, at times, nothing beats the guidance of someone who's been there, as a patient.

A magazine solicited the advice of women who'd had breast cancer and got tips on everything from how to find the best doctor, to informing friends and family, to dealing with hair loss from chemotherapy.

- "Find a doctor who will give you kind words and encouragement," said one woman. Her physician gave facts and hope.
- "Encourage your spouse to tell his friends so he can get support. One person doesn't get cancer, everyone around her does."
- Shave your head. Purchase a wig. "Carry tissues… your nose is going to run a lot more with no hairs in it."

If you've faced illness, divorce, job loss or another crisis, what you've learned can help others.

Give me good counsel and encouragement. (Wisdom of Solomon 8:9)

Assist me in counseling others with the wisdom of experience, Holy Redeemer.

Is It Worth It?

Money can't buy happiness, right? Well, according to a recent study, it may–but only if you have more of it than others.

Researchers at Harvard University found that among the 20,000 people they studied, aged 20- to 64-years old, the size of a person's paycheck mattered only in how it measured up against those of their peers. Those who made more than others in their social group, even if it wasn't much by other standards, seemed to take joy from it.

"Rather than promoting overall happiness, continued income growth could promote an ongoing consumption race where individuals consume more and more, just to maintain a constant level of happiness," said the study's leader.

Should happiness be a competition, though? When life offers us so much more from which to draw happiness, doesn't it make sense to reorient our priorities? Where do you look for happiness?

Happy are the people whose God is the Lord. (Psalm 144:15)

Blessed Paraclete, help me to find genuine happiness in my life.

Nourishing Words

From Genesis to Revelation, the Bible brims with words of guidance, faith, promise and other forms of nourishment. Did you ever think about the many references to physical nourishment—food—in the Bible? Consider these...

Onions, leeks and garlic were important to the Israelites in Egypt and later recognized for their medicinal properties.

Apples are mentioned starting with Genesis' story of Adam and Eve.

Fig trees provide sweet fruit for eating and for crushing into a medicinal poultice. The fig tree is a symbol of fruitful faithfulness.

Olives are an edible, tangy, black, green or purplish fruit. Crushed, olives yield oil for religious rituals, illumination, skin care, medicines, cooking and eating.

God gave us plants for food and for medicines. While recognizing the value of modern medicines, it may also be time to rediscover God's gift of nutritious and healing plants.

(He) gave me unerring knowledge of...the varieties of plants and the virtues of roots. (Wisdom of Solomon 7:17,20)

Divine Physician, help us rediscover and use wisely plants' healing treasures.

Diversity, U. S. Hallmark

When bestselling writer Antwone Fisher was invited to speak with the students of Los Angeles' Marymount High School, he focused on diversity and respect.

Well-known from the 1998 film about his life, Fisher had to deal with a difficult upbringing including sexual abuse. Then he joined the Navy where he learned to rely on and be relied upon by others regardless of background or beliefs.

During his address, Fisher emphasized that "in America like in the Navy we're diverse. That's not true of other "countries...where people are pretty much one race," creed or ethnic group.

Fisher later said about his audience, "They're kids with dreams, and when they leave school they'll learn life is often a struggle with people who are different than they are. My goal was to tell them to try and get along and never give up the dream."

Treat everyone with the respect you demand for yourself.

Pay to all what is due them...respect to whom respect is due, honor to whom honor is due. (Romans 13:7)

Creator, unite the people of the United States in mutual respect and heartfelt tolerance.

Retracting Our Beliefs

Even if we learn something is not true, that does not necessarily mean we stop believing it.

According to Stephan Lewandowsky, a professor of psychology at the University of Western Australia, people who read a retraction of a newspaper story often still accept the original article as true.

Lewandowsky says this is particularly the case when the initial information supports the reader's personal beliefs. He says that "people build mental models. By the time they learn of a retraction, the original misinformation has already become an integral part of that mental model, or worldview, and disregarding it would leave the worldview in shambles."

There's nothing odd about wanting our beliefs to be supported by facts. Yet, we must recognize that wishing does not make something so and that we cannot invent the truth to please ourselves. Be willing to think clearly and judge rationally—and to accept the truth, like it or not.

The Spirit of truth...will guide you into all the truth...because He will take what is Mine and declare it to you. (John 16:13,14)

Spirit of Knowledge, guide me in seeking Your truth wherever it leads me.

The Coffee Crusaders

The town of Wellfleet, Massachusetts, was already reeling from one of the coldest most severe winters in decades, but when its independent coffee shop closed due to escalating costs, it proved to be too much.

"It seemed our town was depressed for months," says writer Kathy Shorr. Many of the town's residents began searching for a way to reopen the town coffee shop. In the process, they discovered a new awareness of community and fellowship. Civic relations began to take on new meaning. They learned "it can be everything from helping out a neighbor to voting at a town meeting," says Shorr.

The Wellfleet town coffee shop has reopened under new ownership. And the lesson Wellfleet learned will likely stand the test of time. Says Shorr, "It boils down to feeling connected to your community."

Community and community service can take many forms. What can you do to improve your neighborhood?

To each is given the manifestation of the Spirit for the common good....wisdom...knowledge... faith...gifts of healing. (1 Corinthians 12:7,8,9)

Remind me, Lord Jesus, that I am not meant to be alone.

Unexpected Bargain

Linda Stafford's hobby of shopping at garage sales had gotten her 30 years of good-natured kidding from her family. After all, who needed all that junk?

The kidding stopped, however, when Stafford tried to move a chair she'd purchased several years earlier at one of those garage sales. When her daughter heard something rattle inside the chair, they removed the chair's bottom and found $3,070 in cash tucked into two envelopes.

The price she'd paid for the chair? $2.00.

If you have a hobby, skill or interest that brings you joy, celebrate it proudly. After all, it could have unexpected dividends, even beyond the pleasure it brings you!

Rejoice with an indescribable and glorious joy. (1 Peter 1:8)

Lord, thank You for all the people who bring me joy. May I, too, offer them joy. And thank You, too, for every thing in Your creation which delights me.

Art Scene? Crime Scene?

Some visitors to New York's famed Frick Museum are not just there to enjoy beautiful art; they are there to be better cops.

Amy Herman, the museum's director of education has been conducting classes for high-ranking police officers since 2004. The program, a spin-off of one begun several years earlier for medical students, has also been taken by FBI agents and London police officers.

Called "The Art of Observation," the program tries to sharpen officers' perceptions to enable them to better solve crimes. "I want them to look at crime scenes more thoroughly and think about the different ways things can happen," says Herman. They look at paintings as diverse as Anthony Van Dyck's portrait of "Frans Snyder" and Claude Lorraine's the "Sermon on the Mount."

Improving our observational skills can also help each of us better appreciate our world and the people around us. Open more than your eyes.

Take the log out of your own eye, and then you will see clearly to take the speck out of your neighbor's eye. (Luke 6:42)

Holy Trinity, guide me in using the talents with which You have blessed me, for my good and that of others.

The Divi Divi Tree

On the Caribbean islands of Aruba, Bonaire and Curacao, there's a tree that grows in the direction of the trade winds. It's called the Divi Divi, or *Watapana* in Arawak.

Instead of growing straight up, its branches yield to the trade winds, permanently swept in one direction.

Much can be learned from the Divi Divi's growth pattern. There are times in our lives when the wind blows us in a different direction from others.

Will we stiffen against it? Do we realize that resisting our path can be as challenging as accepting it? Yet, by accepting it, will we gain the individual shape meant for us?

The Divi Divi beautifies its corner of the world by adapting. May we also adapt, becoming who we are supposed to become; beautifying our corner of God's good earth.

The trees once went out to anoint a king over themselves. So they said to the olive tree, 'Reign over us'. The olive tree answered them 'Shall I stop producing my rich oil...and go to sway over the trees?' (Judges 9:8-9)

Loving Creator, give us the courage to be no more and no less than the beings You created us to be.

Finding Solace for the Journey

Airports are by nature busy, noisy places. But some of them provide a chapel offering quiet and solitude for people of all faiths, or no faith.

The non-denominational Vancouver Airport Chapel, for example, is open 24/7. Bibles in half a dozen languages are available. Muslim guests find the direction of Mecca needed for their daily prayers. Visitors include stranded passengers, refugees and travelers flying because of an emergency or death in the family, as well as airline and airport workers. The chapel is also the site of weddings, memorial services and fear-of-flying seminars.

Head chaplain Rev. Layne Daggett says, "It's a microcosm. People that you see here are reflective of the larger community. They are part of the beautiful mosaic of culture as a whole. And for me it's all part of the daily routine."

We are all travelers. Wherever our journey takes us, let's celebrate the richness of life that God has created.

I am going to send an angel in front of you, to guard you on the way and to bring you to the place that I have prepared. (Exodus 23:20)

Beloved God, thank You for the gifts of prayer and solitude. Enable us to use them to appreciate Your holy presence.

One Person, Two Brains

There's little doubt that it is the brain that enables humans to think and learn. But did you know you actually have a brain within your brain?

Inside the brain is an emotional brain, built differently from the rest of the neo-cortex, which is the center of language and thought.

The emotional brain controls everything that governs physical well-being, as well as much of the body's physiology: for example, the heart, blood pressure and immune system.

It should come as no surprise, then, that research is revealing the amazing capacity of our emotional brain to heal our body. Experts say that the emotional brain contains natural mechanisms for self-healing. Also, human beings constantly strive for a harmonious balance between their two brains.

Balance, harmony and self-healing are principles that should guide every area of our lives. How can you incorporate these into your daily life?

He said..."Come away to a deserted place all by yourselves and rest a while." (Mark 6:31)

Father, remind us of the importance of balance and moderation in life.

Outgrowing Friendships

Writer Robert Lockwood tells about the last time he saw his college buddy Tom, with whom he'd shared more than a few colorful college escapades.

The two had shared some good times in "the old days," but over 30 years later, when Tom asked if he could "crash" on Lockwood's couch and hang out to smoke marijuana, a strange feeling overtook him.

Lockwood realized that he'd moved on, but his friend was stuck in many of the destructive, aimless habits of his youth.

After his friend left, a passerby noticed Lockwood's sad expression. "You look like you just lost your best friend," said the stranger, and Lockwood knew that in fact, he had.

Growing and moving on can mean painful change, as well as leaving friends and acquaintances behind. Yet, they also represent possibility, development and fulfillment.

The road to happiness requires that we focus more on what's ahead than what's behind us.

Forgetting what lies behind and straining forward to what lies ahead, I press on toward the goal. (Philippians 3:14)

God, please endow me with the spiritual strength to overcome negative circumstances.

Children's High Hopes

If parents often have high expectations for their children, children can do the same. When 228 boys and girls aged 8 to 12 were asked how their mothers and fathers should act towards them, these are the basic ideas they agreed on:

- Treat all children with equal affection.
- Never lie to a child.
- There should be comradeship between adults and children.
- Answer questions. Never say, "Don't bother me now."
- Don't blame or punish a child in front of friends.
- Concentrate on a child's good points, not failings.
- Be constant in mood and affection.

Children expect to be treated like the intelligent, if little, people they are. Respect their intelligence, innate curiosity, deep spirituality and humanity for their sake, your own and the world's.

He took a little child...in His arms, (and) He said to them, "Whoever welcomes one such child in My name welcomes Me, and...the One who sent Me." (Mark 9:36-37)

Gentle Jesus, help me welcome children as You did.

Making Positive Changes: Everyone's Job

"Right now two or three percent of the people control changes. Imagine a world where everyone is really a change maker," says Bill Drayton, the chief executive officer of the non-profit Ashoka: Innovators for the Public. A practitioner of what he calls social entrepreneurship, Drayton blends vision with practical planning.

Ashoka projects include inexpensive electricity for Brazilian farmers; small-business loans for poor women; encouraging "the haves" to give land to the "have-nots" in India.

According to *U.S. News & World Report*, Drayton's model of change involves people "who combine the pragmatic and results-oriented methods of a business entrepreneur with the goals of a social reformer."

Drayton tries to be a leader who transforms ideas into reality and inspires others to do the same.

Think about how you could address a problem; then draw up a plan and finally, take the first step.

Do not neglect to do good. (Hebrews 13:16)

Inspire many to address today's pressing problems creatively, Good Shepherd.

Apartment Hunting, Finding Mom

When Ellen Pall moved to New York City, she went to look at an apartment for rent in the Greenwich Village neighborhood. "As soon as I went inside, I felt that this was a place I could live," Pall recalled.

Pall would discover that "comfort feeling" was in her genes: her mother had lived in that same building in the 1930s!

Ellen Pall's move to West 12th Street helped her fill in many details about the mother who died before she could get to know her. (Josephine Blatt Pall had died when her daughter was just seven years old.) Pall was even able to locate her mother's former roommate.

"The fact that my mother opened these doors, passed by this railing, pleases me very much," Pall said.

Life's journey takes us to unexpected places. We need to be always alert and aware to discover the joys along the way.

Tobias went out to look for a man to go with him to Media...and (he) found the angel Raphael... but he did not perceive that he was an angel. (Tobit 5:4)

Send Your angels to be with me and protect me, kind Father.

Finding Serenity

Joss Whedon was certain *Firefly* hadn't had a fair chance.

Whedon had already established himself as a successful television producer. Now his new show, *Firefly*, had been cancelled after only a handful of episodes had been aired, out of their proper order. Heartbroken, Whedon refused to give up.

"I just loved the show too much," he said.

Whedon eventually did the seemingly impossible: He convinced a major Hollywood studio to fund a movie based on a cancelled television series. In September 2005, *Serenity*, the motion picture continuation of *Firefly*, was released to enthusiastic fans and reviews. In the coming months, DVD sales of both the film and the short-lived television series would explode and *Serenity* would place on numerous "best of the year" lists.

Sometimes we have to create our own second chances. Don't let failure stop you from trying again.

Be persistent whether the time is favorable or unfavorable. (2 Timothy 4:2)

Divine Lord, help me to always keep my enthusiasm, even in the face of adversity.

Nuns in Norway

In 1999, 15 years after Ina Andresen had entered the Cistercian monastery of La Coudre in Laval, France, she asked for permission to return to her native Norway to witness to her Catholic faith in that predominantly Lutheran country.

Permission granted, Sister Ina and six American Sisters moved to the Norwegian island of Tautra. Their new neighbors welcomed them with open arms and hearts.

Said one islander, "The arrival of these Sisters changed our lives completely. They became our spiritual anchor and our extended family. When we were ill they prayed for us. When we were happy, they shared our joy."

Sharing life's joys and difficulties is the best way for people of different Christian churches to know the "one true God and Jesus Christ whom He has sent." God loves all faith traditions and peoples of the earth. Let us love them, too.

This is eternal life, that they may know You, the only true God, and Jesus Christ whom You have sent. (John 17:3)

May all our actions, Jesus, be deeply respectful of one another's faith, tradition and culture.

Never Say Never

Lots of people tell you what to do. Writer Sally Stich tells you what never to do:

Never treat friends better than family. Don't take family for granted. Be respectful and pick your battles.

Never be a know-it-all. Listen to others "The world won't stop if you keep some of your knowledge to yourself."

Never miss an opportunity to share a kind word. Sincere compliments can have a ripple effect.

Never sit still when action is called for. Seek support, encouragement, and new ideas.

Never ignore your gut. Pay attention to your feelings and use your intuition.

Never stop learning. New skills and ideas make you more interesting and make you feel good.

Never stop having fun. Fun doesn't have to last for days or be expensive. Even setting aside responsibilities for a brief time is refreshing.

And always seek to do God's will.

Learn where there is wisdom...strength... understanding...length of days and life...light for the eyes, and peace. (Baruch 3:14)

Bless our efforts to be the persons we were created to be, Holy Spirit.

Shoe Shine Hero

Albert Lexie has been shining shoes for almost 50 years. It seems everyone knows him, but not just for his sparkling work.

In 1981, Lexie saw a news report that the Children's Hospital of Pittsburgh was raising money for their Free Care Fund. He decided that helping children get care was important. And so he donated the tips he had saved all year to the hospital—and pledged to do so from then on.

Over the years, shine by shine, those tips have amounted to over $100,000 and a lot of help for kids. When people get a shoe shine from Lexie, they know that good can come from a small job and a big heart.

Each of us can be a true philanthropist by loving and caring for God's people.

Take care that you do not despise one of these little ones; for, I tell you, in heaven their angels continually see the face of My Father in heaven. (Matthew 18:10)

What can we do, Savior, to apply the Gospel to infants and children?

Dollar Coins

We've all had those days when it feels as though the world is crashing down on our shoulders.

One day a young woman was on her way to work. It had been the week from hell. A friend had just died. She was running on three hours of sleep, had tons of work to do for college and, on top of that, was working on a student film. Everything was happening at once. She also had no money to spare.

She arrived at Manhattan's Grand Central two minutes before her train left. She had to buy a ten dollar ticket for the train, but discovered she only had six dollars with her.

The conductor had no sympathy. Kindness, though, was only a seat away. A woman gave her four dollar coins.

Kindness is necessary to all of us. Give it often and accept it with gratitude.

Give graciously to all the living. (Sirach 7:33)

Merciful God, help me to be respectfully kind to others, to myself, to all Your Creation.

Going Green

While Americans are becoming more energy conscious, making use of new technologies, taxes and credits, we're still energy gluttons, writes Jeremiah Creedon in *Utne* magazine. Though people are buying hybrid cars, installing solar roofs and experimenting with wind power, more needs to be done.

"We tend to burn far more energy than people in poorer countries do, and our abundance often comes at their expense," he writes.

Creedon quotes Vaclav Smil, professor at the University of Manitoba and author of *Energy at the Crossroads* that "shaping the future energy use in the affluent world is primarily a moral issue, not a technical or economic matter."

Creedon believes that the bottom line is that if we "stand up for something, others will as well."

Take what steps you can to curb your energy use. Remember that this earth is the home God fashioned for us and gave into our stewardship.

It is required of stewards that they be found trustworthy. (1 Corinthians 4:2)

Show us how to take delight in lives of elegant simplicity, Creator of Heaven and Earth.

How Do You See God?

People who believe in God but think of Him as remote also seem to take a dim view of their own health and have problems with forgiveness.

According to a survey by *Spirituality & Health* magazine of men and women who believe in God, 94 percent describe God as loving and 88 percent said they felt close to God. However, the 22 percent who see God as remote, also saw themselves as more worn out and tired than the others; they also expected their health to get progressively worse.

This same group admitted that they were less likely to forgive themselves or others. And, they're less likely to believe that God forgives them. These same people who view God as remote are more likely to be anxious or depressed than those who feel close to a loving God.

God wants more than our belief. God wants us to rejoice in His boundless love.

When He saw the crowds, (Jesus) had compassion for them, because they were harassed and helpless, like sheep without a shepherd. (Matthew 9:36)

Loving Lord, open my heart to receive the gift of faith in Your compassionate love for me.

Creating Hope for Others

Jeanette Shamblen was 36-years old when she was diagnosed with breast cancer in 1999. A mastectomy, chemotherapy, a stem cell transplant and radiation followed.

Wanting a distraction from the tension and pain, Shamblen turned to watercolor painting. "I was only dabbling, but it felt good," said the wife and mother who worked for an international financial company. She started taking her brushes and paints to her treatments.

This artistic outlet helped her so immensely, she decided to found Creating Hope, a non-profit group that supplies watercolor kits for people dealing with cancer. Though Jeanette Shamblen died in 2003, her gift of encouragement lives on through the volunteers who bring the joy of beauty and creativity to patients.

It's hard to worry about others when we are experiencing pain. Yet, striving to help others, as well as ourselves, can give us peace and purpose.

Why are you cast down, O my soul, and why are you disquieted within me? Hope in God; for I shall again praise Him, my help and my God. (Psalm 42:5-6)

With hope in You, Divine Master, my life is complete—and eternal.

The Important Things

If you find your life getting too complicated, try to stay focused on what's really important. At the end of the day, your relationship with God and with others will always matter far more than anything you own or owe.

Here's how Mother Teresa of Calcutta put it: "Spread love everywhere you go: first of all in your own house. Give love to your children, to your wife or husband, to a next door neighbor. ...

"Let no one ever come to you without leaving better and happier. Be the living expression of God's kindness: kindness in your face, kindness in your eyes, kindness in your smile, kindness in your warm greeting."

No one lacks daily opportunities to offer loving-kindness to someone. Whether they are your family and friends, neighbors and co-workers or total strangers, you can be the bearer of the Lord's blessings to them. Remember, God is never outdone in generosity.

(The) Lord is Lord of all, and is generous to all who call on Him. (Romans 10:12)

Beloved Father, teach me not to worry about trivial things. Help me focus on You and Your gifts of love and life.

Being a Leader

Geoffrey Canada describes what it takes to be a leader: "You have to have a clear vision of what you want to accomplish. Then you have to be able to articulate that vision so others can see it as clearly as you. ...You must simply never give up— even if you doubt at times." Leaders, concludes Canada, must be indefatigable and must not let themselves be afraid.

Canada exemplifies his own words. He heads the Harlem Children's Zone, a program that tends to the educational, health and social services needs of thousands of low-income New York City children. Committed to helping these children from pre-school through college, the educator enlists financial help from friends and others who believe in his goal.

Leadership isn't easy for anyone, but the world needs each of us to use our God-given abilities to do good, especially for those most in need.

May you be made strong with all the strength that comes from His glorious power. (Colossians 1:11)

Guide me, Spirit of Fortitude. Enable me to do simply what You ask of me today—to lead, to follow, to seek Your will.

Getting to the Point

You probably know that there's no lead in a lead pencil, but here are a few other things you may not know about them:

- Graphite, the form of carbon used to make pencils, is named after the Greek word for writing.

- The first hand-glued and planed, wood-cased pencil as well as the first pencil manufacturing company were created by Kaspar Faber in 18th-century Germany.

- Author Henry David Thoreau's father owned a pencil factory in Concord, Massachusetts, and Thoreau actually made several important contributions to the manufacturing process.

- In the 1890's, a high quality pencil maker used the yellow and black colors of the Austro-Hungarian flag, and imitators followed suit.

- A standard number 2 pencil can write almost 50,000 words or draw a line 35 miles long.

Even the simplest things can have interesting histories. Open your mind. Develop your curiosity – and creativity.

Can you bind the chains of the Pleiades...or can you guide the Bear with its children? (Job 38:31,32)

Father of all creation, help me appreciate the riches and power of Your universe – and the riches of human potential.

How Well Do You Work?

Someone, somewhere, benefits by every task that is performed well. Every job has the potential to improve this world. However, it's up to each of us how well our own work is done.

John Gardner, Secretary of Health, Education and Welfare under President Lyndon Johnson, and founder of Common Cause, observed: "The society which scorns excellence in plumbing because plumbing is a humble activity and tolerates shoddiness in philosophy because it is an exalted activity will have neither good plumbing nor good philosophy. Neither its pipes nor its theories will hold water."

Knowing a job is well done is one of the great satisfactions of life. More than that, we owe it to those who depend on us for quality. When others fail to do their best for us, we notice it quickly enough. Let's make an effort to be just as aware of our job's own standards.

All are skillful in their own work. Without them no city can be inhabited. (Sirach 38:31-32)

Holy God, help me be part of Your on-going work of creation by working to the best of my ability.

Children Making A Difference

Daniel Spencer became a 12-year-old philan-thropist to help keep a sibling-support group running at the University Children's Hospital in Irvine, California.

He set up a series of lemonade stands, enlisted a supervising adult for each and several young friends as volunteers. Nicknamed Pucker Up For Kids, the group raised $973.

"It felt so good to be able to help people," said Daniel.

Diana Ayala was 15 when diagnosed with Ewing's sarcoma, a rare cancer of the bones and soft tissues that eventually killed her. While she was still able, she wanted to make an impact on further research into her cancer. She organized a one-day bake sale to raise money. Diana Ayala raised $8,500.

Youngsters often have the necessary persist-ence, passion and compassion to act as catalysts for positive change. Encourage them.

I was overjoyed to find some of your children walking in the truth. (2 John 4)

Abba, remind parents to support their children's good deeds in word and action.

Giving Care, Getting Care

"Baby Boomers" are earning a new nickname, "The Sandwich Generation." Many are caring for aging parents, raising their own children and working full or part time.

Consider these troubling statistics from the Family Caregiver Alliance for 2005: About 44 million American families and friends help someone sick or disabled. Nearly one-quarter of households care for someone over 50. These statistics will continue to grow.

This effort takes a physical, mental and financial toll on those who schedule 24-hour-a-day care for their loved ones, but don't look after themselves.

Terry Team, director of the Waynesboro, Virginia, Daily Living Center, says, "A support network is very important. Family and friends forget they need a break. ...Learn to reach out."

If you're a caregiver ask for support. If you see someone else struggling to care for a loved one, offer your time and help.

Those who honor their father atone for sins, and those who respect their mother are like those who lay up treasure. (Sirach 3:3-4)

Heavenly Father, remind caregivers to share their burdens with others for their own good and the good of their loved ones.

Excuses, Excuses

As author Frank McCourt tells it, when he was a teacher, he was inundated by counterfeit excuse notes. His students never showed as much creativity as they did while trying to pose as their own parents. Fires, evictions, robberies and other disasters played across their pages to excuse absences, latenesses and missed assignments.

McCourt, in a moment of inspiration, made writing excuse notes an assignment for his class. Soon, students who bristled at the thought of writing even a short passage were enthusiastically writing lengthy notes to explain the behavior of Adam and Eve, Julius and Ethel Rosenberg, Attila the Hun, Lee Harvey Oswald and Al Capone.

Rather than cracking down on classes or giving up in frustration, McCourt took advantage of a unique opportunity to teach his students. Inventive thinking and a positive attitude are two traits that need never be excused.

Hope does not disappoint us. (Romans 5:5)

Lord, help me to look at my challenges in a fresh and positive way.

Choose Joy

Some people have the wonderful ability not to let difficult people or tough situations get them down.

Customers at one coffee shop noticed that their waiter was unflappable no matter how busy things got or how rude certain folks could be. When asked how he could stay so positive, no matter what, the waiter said, "I don't let anyone steal my joy. The world didn't give it to me, and the world can't take it away."

Our joy, our happiness is our own. While it's true that people and events affect us, we still get to choose our own perspective on life as well as our beliefs and our feelings.

Television broadcaster Hugh Downs put it this way: "A happy person is not a person in a certain set of circumstances, but rather a person with a certain set of attitudes."

Choose what is right. (Job 34:4)

Bless my heart and make it Yours, my Savior, so that it may fill to overflowing with Your joy.

Building a Dream on Furniture

In 1942, John Johnson secured a $500 loan using his mother's furniture as collateral. He took that money and built a publishing empire–*Ebony* and *Jet* magazines–that is today the number one African-American publishing company in the world.

When he died in 2005, Johnson was remembered by his family and friends as a man of "indomitable spirit who refused to take 'no' for an answer."

For the man who went from a short stint on welfare to the Forbes list of the 400 richest Americans, defying the odds seemed to define his life.

In his autobiography, *Succeeding Against the Odds,* John Johnson offered this message to "dreamers everywhere"–"long shots do come in and hard work, dedication and perseverance will overcome almost any prejudice and open almost any door."

Run with perseverance the race set before us. (Hebrews 12:1)

Give me the strength to persevere, gracious Creator, so that I may do great things in Your name.

From the Ashes...

In the RAF-USAF incendiary bombing of Dresden on February 13-14, 1945 the 200 year old Frauenkirchen, or Church of Our Lady, along with the rest of the city was reduced to heaps of corpses, ash and rubble.

Sixty years later, on October 30, 2005, a rebuilt Frauenkirchen was reconsecrated by Lutheran bishop Jochen Bohl. Bishop Bohl said that the rebuilding of Our Lady's Church "was... in the spirit of reconciliation."

The golden orb and cross atop the lantern was crafted by London goldsmith Alan Smith, the son of an RAF squadron member on the bombing runs. England's Duke of Kent was also present. And British citizens contributed generously toward the $120 million cost of the rebuilding.

The rebuilding of this church is a reminder that reconciliation is a long, yet moment by moment reestablishment of peace with others, with God, even with one's own imperfect self.

If...your brother or sister has something against you...be reconciled to your brother or sister. (Matthew 5:23,24)

God, nations commit atrocities during war. Forgive us. Extirpate violence from our midst.

Making Valentine's Day "Love Day"

Who says Valentine's Day is only for couples? Parents and children can create a family celebration of love. Try these ideas:

- Set the dinner table with red and heart-shaped items.
- Have everyone in the family wear red to dinner.
- Serve red foods such as tomatoes, red peppers or cranberry juice. Or bake homemade heart-shaped cookies.
- Ask family members what they love about one another.
- Talk about your marriage or the grandparents'– and not just the joys and good times. Mention spouses aging together.
- Talk about God's unconditional love for each member of the family and for all of His children everywhere.

Together, a family can have a heartfelt celebration of love on St. Valentine's Day and every day.

If I...do not have love, I am a noisy gong or a clanging cymbal. ...I am nothing. ...I gain nothing. Love never ends. (1 Corinthians 13:1,2,3,8)

Abba, O Father, remind me that love is Your law for right relationships.

Coping with Grief

People marveled at how Coach Matt Ballard of Morehead State University in Kentucky held up under his grief after his 21-year-old son was killed when his motorcycle and a pickup truck crashed.

Memories of his son and the love and support of players, colleagues, friends and family helped. Involvement in football distracted him from his loss. Too, Ballard's strong religious faith sustained him.

"We're going to miss the daylights out of him," Ballard said of his son. "It hurts like crazy. I can't even explain the hurt and the heartache. But the Good Lord didn't promise us it was going to be easy. He did promise that, 'I'm going to be with you.'"

Coping with grief is a painful process which can be eased by the knowledge that we are not alone. Who needs that support from you?

As He approached (Nain)...a man who had died was being carried out. He was his mother's only son, and she was a widow...the Lord...had compassion for her and...gave him to his mother. (Luke 7:12,13,15)

Who needs my compassion in their grief, Lord of Life?

From the Heart

Do you believe there is such thing as a sixth sense? Nancy Rosanoff, a consultant and teacher, says that "sometimes what we call intuition is simply admitting to ourselves things we have long known or felt in our hearts."

She suggests writing and repetition as good ways to get in touch with our selves. Here's an exercise she gives students:

1. Write down a specific concern; perhaps a work issue or a relationship concern.
2. Below it write, "I know in my heart..." and finish the thought with whatever comes naturally to mind about your concern.
3. Write the phrase again and finish the sentence with another response that occurs to you immediately. Repeat ten times.

Your finished product, which may read like a poem, a litany or a refrain, may help connect you to your truest feelings.

Next time you have a troubling concern, listen to your intuition, to your deepest self.

You know how to interpret the appearance of the sky, but you cannot interpret the signs of the times. (Matthew 16:3)

Holy Spirit, teach me how to interpret the signs of the times both internally and externally.

In Him We Are Strong

"A chronic illness can be incredibly lonely and isolating. But I refused to let it rob me of the joy of living," says Maureen Pratt. The Santa Fe, California, woman fights to live a life of beauty.

Pratt was diagnosed with lupus, a serious chronic illness which has altered her life. But she has the support of family and friends as well as a strong faith to keep her going. She also has a hobby she loves, gardening. While everyday is a struggle for her, she says she is grateful: "I believe God is with me. And he is closest to me when I am deepest in my pain."

We can learn from Maureen Pratt to focus on God at all times. In His presence, we can find the source peace, no matter how difficult or painful our lives may be.

He said to me, 'My grace is sufficient for you, for power is made perfect in weakness'. So I will boast all the more gladly of my weaknesses, so that the power of Christ may dwell in me." (2 Corinthians 12:9)

Compassionate God, help me hold on to Your promise and remain faithful to You through good times and difficult ones.

Rappin' on the F Train

Angelo Stagnaro was riding the train and reading St. Teresa of Avila when a group of young men "replete with do-rags...gaudy jewelry...and dirty jeans pulled halfway down their rear ends..." boarded.

Though they looked like "everyone's worst nightmare," as Stagnaro wrote in *National Catholic Reporter,* he helped them find their destination on a subway map, and found them to be friendly and thankful. When one of them asked him about his book, Stagnaro learned that the men were Catholic rappers.

The discussion continued for the rest of their ride together. Afterwards, Stagnaro listened to some of the young men's recordings and appreciated both their message and their musicianship.

And so, from an encounter that he initially assumed would be negative, Stagnaro found himself with a new appreciation for both rap music and for his own religion.

Keep an open mind–you never know where you might discover inspiration and enlightenment.

Judge your neighbor's feelings by your own. (Sirach 31:15)

Lord, help me to keep an open mind and to not make unfounded judgments.

The Difficult Side of Leadership

Public figures whose opinions are based on polls or popular views do not understand genuine leadership. Consider Eleanor Roosevelt's championing of the African-American contralto Marian Anderson in 1939.

Anderson had been invited by Howard University to sing at the Daughters of the American Revolution (DAR) owned Constitution Hall. The DAR refused to rent its hall to African-Americans.

Appalled, Eleanor Roosevelt resigned from the DAR. In an open letter she wrote that they had wasted the chance "to lead in an enlightened way." Next, the First Lady arranged for her friend Marian Anderson to sing on the steps of the Lincoln Memorial. Lastly, she chose not to attend the concert lest her presence detract from Marian Anderson's singing or triumph.

How often do public figures show such courage? Do you remind them to do so? Do you show such courage yourself?

In passing judgement on another you condemn yourself. (Romans 2:1)

Spirit of Courage, guide leaders and all of us in doing what is right.

Sharing Food with Friends

Evelyn Hamann was lonely in a big city. Newly married to her college sweetheart, Scott, she'd moved to his hometown of Spokane, Washington. Other than his family, she knew no one.

"'Lord,' I prayed one day," she recalls, "I need a friend.'" After that prayer, she decided to prepare her family's dinner favorite, pasties, hearty pies stuffed with meat, potatoes and rutabaga.

She almost prepared pasties again the next week when Scott's friend Glen and his wife Tracy came to dinner, but she chose burgers instead. While doing the dishes, Evelyn told Tracy that she almost made another meal, a favorite in her Montana family. Before Evelyn could name the dish, Tracy spoke of a number one choice in her own family's home-pasties.

"Thank you, Lord," Evelyn thought. She had found a friend.

Prayers are answered in God's time.

A thousand years in Your sight are like yesterday when it is past, or like a watch in the night. (Psalm 90:4)

We are human, Loving Father. Help us be patient until You answer our prayers in the way You know best.

When You Fast This Lent

Are you "giving up" something for Lent? That's fine as long as it's truly pertinent to your life.

Sr. Melannie Svoboda, SND, author of *Abundant Treasures,* suggests developing a healthy spirituality. "Our fasting during Lent should be integral to our daily living," she says. "Some people choose to do only 'tacked-on' penances that are extraneous to their lives. A workaholic, for example, gives up chocolate for Lent. Wouldn't it be more fitting to 'fast' from work and spend more time with family?

"Healthy penance flows from our relationships, responsibilities and religious convictions. Some examples are: to drive compassionately, to be patient with coworkers, to be kinder to store clerks, to visit an elderly relative or friend, to be honest, to slow down, to extend forgiveness...to count blessings."

Lent is an intensified opportunity to grow in holiness in some little way every day. Only never let yourself fast or abstain from joy.

Rejoice in the Lord always; again I will say, Rejoice. (Philippians 4:4)

Beloved Redeemer, help me give up all that separates me from You and to embrace all that draws me closer to You.

This Ventriloquist was No Dummy

You may remember Paul Winchell, the voice of Tigger in *Winnie the Pooh* cartoon features for more than three decades.

Others may remember Winchell's 1940s television debut as a ventriloquist in *The Paul Winchell-Jerry Mahoney Show*, which began his over 60-year long career.

On face value, one might categorize Winchell, who died in 2005, as simply an entertainer. Truth be told, Winchell was much more than that. He wrote books, hosted variety shows, and was an inventor who held 30 patents, including one for an early artificial heart which he built in 1963 and donated to research.

People are complex. Beware simplistic generalizations. There's much more to each person than meets the eye.

Do not judge by appearances. (John 7:24)

Jesus, help me to avoid stereotypes and to respect the unique individuality of others.

Treasuring Time's Treasures

Since 1951, when his father bought the high-valley Range Creek ranch, a year seldom passed in which Waldo Wilcox did not come upon some thing of archeological interest: caches of arrowheads; rock-wall drawings; ancient dwellings; occasionally, even burial plots.

For nearly a half century, he kept quiet about his treasures, hidden in the isolated valley 160 miles southeast of Salt Lake City, Utah.

But, when ranching was no longer an option, the then 75-year-old Wilcox sold his ranch to a national conservation group, revealing his secret treasury of Native American history. Today, archeologists are busy cataloguing magnificent, previously unknown ruins on the property–now at 300 and counting. "I suspect we'll find 10 times that number," says Kevin Jones, Utah's head state archeologist.

Finds such as these remind us that we can learn from the ways and wisdom of those who have gone before us.

Let us now sing the praises of...our ancestors... who...made a name for themselves. (Sirach 44:1,3)

You shower us with uncountable blessings, Holy Spirit. Thank You.

Motivating Yourself

If you're like so many others, getting out of bed five mornings a week to start the workday seems closer to drudgery than a fresh start to a new day. One manager who'd always worked in regimented office environments found he couldn't focus once he began working from home.

He decided he needed a daily ritual. Every morning, he'd walk out his front door, turn right, and walk around the block to his "office." At day's end, he reversed the procedure.

Although he was literally walking in circles, his new habit injected fresh discipline into his day and helped him regain a sense of order.

What routines guide your day? How do they help motivate you? Can you improve them?

Whatever your hand finds to do, do with your might. (Ecclesiastes 9:10)

Renew my spirit and my attitude with a fresh and positive perspective, Divine Master, so that I may fulfill my obligations.

Accepting God's Mission

The Christophers has always believed that each one of us has been entrusted by God with a mission that only we can fulfill.

Ask yourself what God wants you to accomplish, then consider these thoughts from Rev. James McKarns, writing in *Living Faith:* "If we can see our lives as being on a mission, it will give us strength and courage far beyond that which we previously though we possessed. When there is a cause and purpose for us to achieve, we are energized and we proceed in haste to see it fulfilled.

"Our plan to bring a dream to reality may often seem very difficult, but if it's true and good, then we also need to remember that 'nothing is impossible with God.'"

Pray that your plans will be true and good–God's plans–and that He will guide each step along the way. Trust yourself to God's will.

Search me, O God, and know my heart; test me and know my thoughts. ...and lead me in the way everlasting. (Psalm 139:23,24)

I want to live Your will, Merciful Father. Help me trust You.

How To Think Big

For writer and educator Janet Ruth Falon, thinking big isn't a matter of money or fame. "It's about acting in ways that push you beyond the boundaries of your own basic needs and that plug your life into the larger picture of the universe."

She offers these suggestions:

- Look for ways to step out of your normal routine and connect with others. Compliment a stranger. Show an interest in your neighbor's garden or pets.
- Have friends of all ages and appreciate their different perspectives.
- Learn names. Not just of people, but of the birds, flowers and other living things. It's a much richer experience to say, "There's a nuthatch," than, "There's a cute little bird."
- Keep a journal and tune into your soul.
- Reconnect with old friends and acquaintances.
- Grow big in spirit by giving your time or money to charitable causes.

Connect. Re-connect. Think big.

All things work together for good for those who love God. (Romans 8:28)

Push me to get involved, to be concerned, to be active in whatever way possible, in my community and the world, Holy Spirit.

Keeping Hope Alive

Artist Robert Shetterly believes that "truth comes with lots of different faces."

The veteran civil rights activist thought about Walt Whitman's words: "Love the earth and sun and the animals, despise riches, give alms... stand up for the stupid and crazy, devote your income and labor to others, hate tyrants, argue not concerning God, have patience and indulgence toward the people, take off your hat to nothing."

This led to "Americans Who Tell the Truth," portraits of those who championed the deepest freedoms: Martin Luther King, Jr., Susan B. Anthony, Abraham Lincoln, Henry David Thoreau, Jane Addams, Mother Jones and Chief Joseph, for example. He etched a quotation from each onto their portrait.

Shetterly says, "I am using democracy in its best sense as being a fundamental truth that gives dignity and equal worth to every individual."

In your home, neighborhood and country, seek truth and justice–and encourage others to do the same.

Proclaim liberty throughout the land to all its inhabitants. (Leviticus 25:10)

Inspire and protect our efforts to return our nation to its foundational values, God of Justice.

Good Vacations

People usually go on vacation hoping they'll get good service. Some, however, plan vacations during which they can be of service. In her *Catholic Digest* article, Judi Dash wrote of the increasing number of families who

- renovate houses for the elderly poor
- work on American Indian reservations
- execavate cultural and historical sites to preserve our historical memory
- clear hiking trails in state or national parks
- rebuild arson–burned churches

Initially some teens told their parents they didn't want to go on a service vacation, preferring traditional vacations instead.

But in the end they appreciated the value of serving. "It made me feel I was needed and could make a difference in someone's life," said a 15-year-old.

Might this be the year your family takes a vacation to serve rather than to be served?

The Son of Man came not to be served but to serve. (Mark 10:45)

Inspire many families to use their vacation time to help others or to discover and preserve tangible evidence of the past.

Giving Yourself Away

If you find yourself tired-out and bored from your daily routine, you are not alone.

In Ohio, a successful automobile dealer has come up with a way to put new enthusiasm in his work and life. Every morning he chooses a small gift, say a pen or even a few dollars, to give away during the day. Then he stays alert to find the person who will receive the present.

It might be an employee or customer, or just someone he meets who seems to deserve some special recognition. He says, "By constantly searching for the opportunity to give, I have a wonderful day."

People who give of themselves not only improve their chances of having a wonderful day, they help others have a happier day as well. Nurture your own generosity–it just might be the best gift you ever give yourself.

As for those who...are rich, command them...to do good, to be rich in good works, generous, and ready to share...so that they may take hold of the life that really is life. (1 Timothy 6:17,18,19)

Dear Lord, You give us everything, even Yourself. Encourage us to imitate Your generosity.

Hearts at Home in the Bronx

They've come from France–a college student, an executive, a nun and a computer programmer–to establish a prayerful presence in the Highbridge neighborhood of The Bronx, New York.

"Our mission is to bring friendship and consolation to people who suffer," explains Cyril Rabeisen, who has taken a year's leave from his job at an energy company.

Heart's Home, a Catholic program that has existed since 1990, now has communities in 20 countries worldwide. Prayer is a big part of the Bronx group's presence. A daily Rosary procession takes them through busy commercial strips and past small grocery stores, fast-food joints and apartment buildings.

Rev. Michael Sepp, pastor of two local Catholic churches, says, "Their quiet prayer presence has a much greater effect than we realize."

Being with others in their neediness is far more important than anything we can say.

Abide in Me as I abide in you. ...I am the vine, you are the branches. (John 15:4,5)

You abide with us in our neediness as well as in our good times, Jesus. Enable us to abide with others in good times and bad.

Nurturing the Family Tree

Edith Wagner likes to bring families together.

The author of *The Family Reunion Source Book* and editor of *Reunions* magazine has some suggestions for anyone hoping to gather in celebration with far-flung extended family.

- About a year before, send a save-the-date card. Follow up with flyers or E-mail.
- Plan to have mementoes such as personalized mugs or T-shirts.
- Use a caterer unless the family prefers potluck.
- Schedule activities such as golf or heritage tours. Don't forget a variety of fun and games for the youngsters.
- Find creative ways to defray expenses.

And don't worry too much about feuding family members. If they don't attend "that's their loss," says Wagner. On the other hand a reunion "is the perfect place to mend fences and build bridges."

> **(God) reconciled us to Himself through Christ, and has given us the ministry of reconciliation. (2 Corinthians 5:18)**

Give success to efforts to resolve family feuds, Father.

Where God Is

Laura Knight Moretz' son Thomas and his best friend Josh both attended the Temple Emanuel Preschool. But when the 3-year-old started asking questions about religious differences, she wondered how to explain things.

Writing in *Guideposts* magazine, Moretz, a Presbyterian, recounts that she told Thomas, "You know Josh and his family go to Temple Emanuel? "Well, our church and the synagogue have the same God, just different beliefs about Jesus."

A few days later, the little boy asked her, "Mama, where God is? Where God is?"

"You tell me, Thomas. Where is God?"

He laughed and answered, "God is in my heart. ...The rabbi told me."

Moretz hugged her son, saying, "He's a smart guy. And so are you, Thomas."

Faith in God is a tremendous gift—and so is knowing that God is big enough to fill all hearts.

Those of steadfast mind You keep in peace—in peace because they trust in You. Trust in the Lord forever, for in the Lord God you have an everlasting rock. (Isaiah 26:3-4)

Eternal God, source of all love, help us to respect others' faith in Your presence and action in their lives and ours'.

A Tree Grows in Nebraska

One would think that children living in Nebraska would know all there is to know about farming and nature. But Mike Hillis, a Nebraska florist, knew that this was not the case in his own town.

"Many of our kids had only seen vegetables in the supermarket, packaged and wrapped in plastic," he says. "I felt that something important was missing from their lives.

Hillis set out to raise enough money to launch an educational community project that would help kids learn the wonders of nature through hands-on experience. The result: an expansive garden and science/nature-learning center that offers youngsters a chance to plant seeds and evaluate the results.

Putting ideas into action takes time, courage and perseverance. The results, however, can bloom into wonderful gifts for many.

God said, "See, I have given you every plant yielding seed...and every tree with seed in its fruit; you shall have them for food." (Genesis 1:29)

Help me see my useful ideas to fruition, Creator of all.

Lo Mein or Spaghetti?

There's nothing more Italian than pasta and noodles, right?

Maybe not. It's long been contended that noodles were first brought to Italy from China by Marco Polo, although that particular story is highly disputed. Records of Italian noodles predate Polo's journey to the East.

There is some evidence, however, that might back up the "imported noodle" claim, even if Polo wasn't the source–archeologists have recently found 4,000-year old noodles near the Yellow River in northwestern China. The petrified noodles, made from millet and found in an overturned, sealed bowl, are the oldest form of noodle ever found.

While this doesn't solve the dispute as to whether noodles were brought to Italy or if they were simply invented there as well, it does put a new twist on a common food item.

The world is full of wonderful surprises. What else may not be quite what it seems if you take a closer look at it?

The wisdom of the scribe depends on...leisure. (Sirach 38:24)

Spirit of Knowledge, help me always to have an active interest in the world around me.

Homes of Their Dreams

Professional football player Warrick Dunn remembers that his mother never got to live her dream. A police officer raising six children on her own, she wanted to own a home. But she was killed during an attempted robbery.

Dunn began Homes for the Holidays in his mother's memory. Since his rookie year in the NFL in 1997, he has made it possible for 52 single moms and their children to move into their own homes. Dunn provides the funding for the down payment and furnishings.

"When we show them their new homes, they jump up and down and give me a big squeeze," he says. "I've seen teenage boys, not just the girls, cry. When that happens, you know you've made a difference in a family's life."

Dreams can come true. Allow love to inspire your actions.

Love one another as I have loved you. (John 15:12)

Thank You, Heavenly Father, for all the blessings in my life—family and friends, most of all.

Cathartic Creativity

"I've never come across a single person who wasn't creative in some way," says Julia Cameron, author of *Walking in This World: The Practical Art of Creativity.*

She also believes that people don't often think of creativity as being a spiritual issue, but it is. Being creative is simultaneously an active form of mediation and prayer. "Any creative action is an act of faith," she says

Creative motivation gives people a sense of insight, makes them more confident in their decision-making, and emboldens them to try new things. Look around and see how different we all are—God was certainly creative. We should be too.

Dance. Draw. Write. Sing. Read. Paint. Travel. Run. Walk. Cook. Play. Go to a museum. Play a sport. Learn a new language. Make creativity a vital part of your life.

We are what He has made us, created in Christ Jesus for good works, which God prepared beforehand to be our way of life. (Ephesians 2:10)

Loving Lord, allow me to use my gifts to change my world.

Moms on the Run

Ori Munson is suited up in running clothes, watching the clock. Soon, she'll strap her drowsy three-year-old into a red jogging stroller–and be off, taking her daily four-mile jog to her daughter Iris' school.

Munson is one of many stay-at-home moms who are part of Mothers Across America, a New York-based running group that aims to combat maternal depression. They encourage isolated, harried mothers all over the city to suit up and lace up, and literally run around town to pick up their children from school.

Munson uses the trip to carve out a bit of time for herself.

Says her daughter Iris, "I like to run because my mom and me can do races together on the sidewalk to school."

No matter the activity, "being" with loved ones–really being with them–accomplishes more than just "doing."

My wife Anna earned money at women's work. (Tobit 2:11)

God, remind us that stay-at-home moms need adult companionship, mental stimulation, exercise and help with child-care and housework.

Take a Guess

What is it that walks with four legs in the morning, with two legs at midday, and with three legs when the sun has gone down?

According to Greek mythology, the Sphinx asked Oedipus this famous riddle while he was traveling to Thebes. Oedipus gave the right answer: a human being–who crawls on all fours as a baby, walks upright on two legs in middle age, but needs a cane in old age.

Phil Cousineau, author of *Riddle Me This,* says that riddles, also called enigmas, conundrums, and teasers, "are simply ingenious questions in search of clever answers."

Popular throughout history in many countries, in today's society they are generally left to children. That's too bad, because, as Aristotle said, reaching "the solution is an act of learning."

Use your imagination and intelligence creatively. You'll have fun along the way.

The Lord created human beings out of earth... and a mind for thinking He gave them. He filled them with knowledge and understanding. (Sirach 17:1, 6-7)

Holy Spirit, guide me in using all the gifts of body, mind and soul with which You have blessed me.

Moved By God's Guidance and Grace

God's grace can "transform anyone into anything, from a murderer to a monk, or a marketer into a published author at the ripe old age of 72. Grace is the key. It can unlock the door of any prison," writes Paul Everett.

In his twenties, Everett felt spiritually restless. A friend nudged him into the ministry. After decades Everett went on retreat to a monastery where he met Brother Jim.

Brother Jim had grown up horribly abused. He married, but at age 20, thinking that his wife, like everyone else in his life, would leave him, he murdered her. He served 20 years in prison and, Everett notes, with God's grace got "through the guilt and the horror...and into the holy light of forgiveness."

Everett found new purpose as the monk's biographer and wrote *The Prisoner: An Invitation to Hope*.

God's transforming grace changes everyone who lets it.

The grace of God and the free gift in the grace of the one man, Jesus Christ, abounded for the many....The free gift following many trespasses brings justification. (Romans 5:15,16)

Drench us with Your grace, Blessed Trinity.

Make the Most of Mistakes

Cicero, the Roman statesman, orator and philosopher, developed a list of six major mistakes that people often make during the course of their lives:

1. The delusion that personal gain is made by crushing others.
2. The tendency to worry about things that cannot be changed or corrected.
3. Insisting that a thing is impossible because we cannot accomplish it.
4. Refusing to set aside trivial preferences.
5. Neglecting development and refinement of the mind, and not acquiring the habit of reading and studying.
6. Attempting to compel others to believe and live as we do.

Whatever mistakes we make, let's recognize them, admit them and learn from them. Then, even failures won't be wasted.

The law of the Lord is perfect...true and righteous...sweeter also than honey.
(Psalm 19:7,9,10)

Let my faults and weaknesses turn into good through Your mercy and my efforts, Spirit of Knowledge.

Good Prayers Make Good Neighbors

Dr. Walter Larimore was a young physician when he and his wife Barb learned that their baby Kate had cerebral palsy. Writing in *Guideposts* magazine, he says that he was so angry that he couldn't pray.

Then the family moved into a new home in Bryson, North Carolina, and met the many neighbors who would change their lives. A couple who lived across the street had no grandchildren and "hoped God would send a family with a little one!" Another couple were empty-nesters "praying to get a young mother for a neighbor." The pastor of the local church told the Larimores about plans for a support group for parents of handicapped children.

The community helped Dr. Larimore see his "daughter as the incredible gift she was. At a time when I couldn't pray, my new neighbors were saying all the prayers I needed."

Prayers and deeds change lives. Turn faith into action.

Open Your eyes, O Lord, and see...the person who is deeply grieved. (Baruch 2:17,18)

Loving Redeemer, teach me to pray not just for myself and my loved ones but for all who need You—and me.

Give Trust, Earn Trust

Whether at home, in our community or on the job, trust is a big part of any relationship.

One company realized that after they took over a smaller firm. The bigger company made an effort to make their new employees feel welcome. Since they honored their own 25-year veterans by engraving their names on bricks and displaying these at headquarters, they wanted to do the same for the workers they had just acquired.

Unfortunately, the smaller company did not have accurate records for all their longtime workers. Top executives discussed how they could resolve the problem. Finally, one said, "It's easy. If employees say they have been here 25 years, believe them. Order the bricks."

Don't neglect to show your faith in those who have earned it through their loyalty. Do your best to be worthy of that loyalty.

Cursed are those who trust in mere mortals... Blessed are those who trust in the Lord...They shall be like a tree planted by water. (Jeremiah 17:5,7-8)

Blessed Trinity, may faith, hope and love grow in my soul.

Children in the Larger Community

Responsibility for raising children in Native American culture does not lie solely with the parents. Rather, grandparents, aunts and uncles and other relatives play an important part. As a result, children grow up with a strong cultural identity, a strength that is lacking in some other cultures.

Helping to care for a grandchild, niece, nephew or younger cousin can bring great fulfillment. Children need role models of healthy teens and adults other than their parents.

Also, time spent with children can bring rewards. Children have a way of traveling a surer route to joy, taking wonder in the simplest things—something adults often have a difficult time doing.

If you have young relatives, commit to spending time with them. You each need each others' example.

Receive the kingdom of God as a little child. (Mark 10:15)

Lead us, Lord, as we strive both to be role models for the young and to see the world with their eyes.

Always Bear in Mind...

Lyle Simpson was on a Bible retreat in 2005 when, during a hike in the woods, a bear began to chase him.

Though most sources recommend that you not run from an attacking bear, a terrified Simpson did just that.

"I was thinking perhaps that I should play dead or climb a tree, but all I could do is run," he later told reporters.

In his flight, Simpson tripped, and the bear was on top of him. It seemed that there was nothing that could save him.

In those dire circumstances, Simpson's martial arts training kicked in, and he walloped the bear with a direct kick to the nose. The startled ursine retreated, leaving Simpson wounded, but alive.

Quick thinking can sometimes make up for even the most grievous mistakes. Always keep your wits about you, and never give up hope.

Like a roaring lion or a charging bear is a wicked ruler over a poor people. (Proverbs 28:15)

Give me the strength to always keep trying, Divine Master, no matter what stands against me.

Honoring St. Patrick

Do you celebrate St. Patrick's Day? How? By reading poetry by Ireland's poets? Listening to traditional Irish music? Attending a parade?

Or, do you offer prayers attributed to St. Patrick and so celebrate Celtic spirituality? Here's part of St. Patrick's "Lorica" or "Breastplate:" "Christ with me/Christ before me/Christ behind me/Christ within me/Christ beneath me/Christ above me/Christ at my right/Christ at my left/...Christ in the heart of everyone who thinks of me/Christ in the mouth of everyone who speaks to me/Christ in every eye that sees me,/ Christ in every ear that hears me."

Honor St. Patrick today: cultivate a deep spirituality and a deep caring for Creation, the work of God's hand.

A bishop must be above reproach, married only once, temperate, sensible, respectable, hospitable, an apt teacher, not a drunkard, not violent but gentle, not quarrelsome, and not a lover of money. (1 Timothy 3:2-3)

Grace your church with deeply spiritual clergy, Jesus.

Enjoying Lenten Pretzels

During Lent, a time of preparation for the celebration of Jesus' resurrection on Easter, early Christians did not drink milk or eat butter, cheese, eggs, cream or meat.

They did make pretzels, however. The rolls, made from water, flour and salt, were shaped in the form of two arms crossing over themselves as a reminder that Lent was a time for prayer. These breads were called "little arms" (*bracellae*). From this Latin word came the German word *bretzel*, which ultimately became our pretzel.

The earliest description of a pretzel, from the fifth century, can be found in the Vatican Library. The French add to that history, claiming the food was developed by a seventh-century monk who called it *pretiola*.

Pretzels remind us that ordinary things contain a spark of the divine.

Jesus said to them, "I am the bread of life. Whoever comes to Me will never be hungry, and whoever believes in Me will never be thirsty." (John 6:35)

Bread of Life, feed us, slake our thirst, that we may be Your faithful disciples.

Pray Where You Are

If you think that you need to be in church or on your knees to pray, think again.

Catholic Digest magazine asked readers to tell them where and when they prayed. A woman from New Jersey sits on her porch in good weather, praying while watching the sunset and listening to "birds, cicadas, crickets, and children all making their 'joyful noise'."

A woman from an Arizona retirement community sits in the outdoor whirlpool and "pray the rosary, using each tree like a bead. I feel the spirit of God all around me."

Others spoke about praying on the check-out line in stores. They pray for patience as well as for others standing there; tired children and fussy babies; those struggling to write checks because of failing eyesight or trembling hands.

We can always find a time and place to draw close to God. The time: now. The place: here.

(Jesus) went up the mountain by Himself to pray. (Matthew 14:23)

Just knowing that You want me to talk with You makes it easier to open my heart, Loving Friend.

A Tale of Two Sisters

Growing up poor in a family of twelve, Mary and Sandra Smithson didn't have much. "But we had the important things: food, shelter and love," says Mary. Her sister, who became a Catholic nun, agrees, adding that their parents stressed education.

When the two, both teachers, saw children failing school in kindergarten and first grade in their hometown of Nashville, they decided to do something. In 2003, Mary Smithson-Craighead and Sister Sandra Smithson began the Smithson-Craighead Academy.

The school takes a simple approach: teach students the basic skills needed for school success in an environment that loves, nurtures and respects every child. "We want people to see these children as lovable and capable of learning," says Sister Sandra.

And they are doing just that.

Great things can be accomplished with good teachers and a lot of love.

Beloved, let us love one another, because love is from God. (1 John 4:7)

Teach me to love as You do, Father, completely and without prejudice.

Feather Weight

Birds migrating up and down the East Coast each spring and fall need to store up energy to continue flying.

"They can really increase their body mass by sometimes 20 percent or more in one or two days," explains Chad Seewagen of the Wildlife Conservation Society in New York. "That's like you or me putting on 40 pounds in two days."

He and others monitor the city's parks as effective "restaurants" for our flying friends. They visit birds' nests and weigh birds.

After checking one winged tourist and finding his weight right for flying, Conservation Society worker Eric Slayton noted, "I bet that bird leaves tonight. He's ready."

We who travel on foot, not by feathered wings, could also use a little help getting ready for life's journeys. A heaping helping of faith, hope and love is the perfect daily diet for each of us.

Look at the birds of the air; they neither sow nor reap nor gather into barns, and yet your heavenly Father feeds them. (Matthew 6:26)

What joy to hear birdsong; to wonder at the colors and patterns of birds' feathers; to admire their flight! Thank You, Lord.

Calls—and Answers

The title character in *Joan of Arcadia,* a television show that aired a few years back, is an ordinary sixteen-year-old who is pursued by God in the guise of everyday people: the cafeteria lady at school, a cute guy her age, a little girl on a playground.

Through these individuals, God coaxes Joan to help those she wouldn't have elected to help—a stuttering classmate on the school's debate team, for example. Joan's actions are often met with suspicion by family and friends. Because of this, Joan struggles with her obedience to God and the frustration of being misunderstood because of that obedience.

We, too, hear God's whispers through the people around us. Even when it's hard to see God's will for us, our family, friends, neighbors, and strangers can often bring us closer to Him.

Has the Lord as great delight in burnt offerings and sacrifices, as in obeying the voice of the Lord? Surely, to obey is better than sacrifice, and to heed than the fat of rams. (1 Samuel 15:22)

Beloved God, help us discern your will for our lives even as we let go of our need to be understood by family and friends.

Feeling Good About Junking Your Junk!

Drowning in clutter? Try "de-cluttering." Here's how:

- Stick to one clutter-busting job at a time. Otherwise, you'll have a string of half-finished projects.

- Timing matters. Throw out things as soon as you've determined they're junk. Otherwise you might hold on to them.

- Keep good company. Involve family or friends. An objective eye is helpful, as is the company.

- Think about others. Ask yourself if you'll need the item in a few years. If not, donate it to a thrift shop for someone else's use.

Letting go of things can be freeing, stimulating growth and change. In our prayer lives, letting go of distractions frees us to better focus on God.

In returning and rest you shall be saved; in quietness and in trust shall be your strength. (Isaiah 30:15)

Help me simplify my life, Master, that I might better appreciate what is of lasting value.

A Neighborhood Needs Flowers

We need not be helpless in the face of traumatic events.

Takeo Lee Wong was distressed by news of the 2005 bus and subway bombings in Britain and was shocked into doing something good and useful in his own New York neighborhood.

"You always think of the strangest things in a moment of crisis," he said. "And when the bombings happened, I thought to myself, I'd really like to see some flowers this summer."

Wong started small. He planted a few lavender and white impatiens and geraniums outside his ground-floor apartment. Noticing how the beauty of the flowers had a positive impact on his neighbors, he planted near their buildings as well.

Now neighbors chat with one another outdoors in an area with a riot of colors, and pleasing fragrances—and new life.

The flowers appear on the earth; the time of singing has come, the voice of the turtledove is heard in the land. The fig tree puts forth its figs, and the vines are in blossom.
(Song of Solomon 2:12,13)

Eternal God, may peace with justice—as well as flowers—bloom in war scarred nations!

Be a Joy-Maker!

Do you sometimes feel you're living life in black-and-white, instead of vivid color? Get the joy back in your life with these simple "joy-making" rules.

- **Grab hold of the "holy instant."** Be present in the moment. Live for the now. Don't get distracted by past mistakes or lists of things to do in the future.

- **Have a vision of the life you want.** Even thinking about setting goals and starting projects to reach them means that you've opened the door to the lifelong joy of continuing achievement.

- **Say something nice to yourself, about yourself.** Say positive, affirming things about yourself. Take joy in being the person you were created to be.

In the end, remembering that you are loved by God gives you reason to rejoice every day.

Rejoice. Let your gentleness be known to everyone. The Lord is near. (Philippians 4:4-5)

Your tender love for me, Creator, gives me every reason to rejoice. Thank You.

Bridges Over Troubled Waters

For Jim Gladson, a day of sailing means a day at sea with at-risk Los Angeles teenagers trying to inspire them to change.

Many of Gladson's crew have never seen the ocean. When they leave their violent neighborhoods, they enter a classroom where teamwork is essential to survival.

"As a society, we need to genuinely recognize the nature of this problem that we're all moaning about," says Gladson. "What do you do with dysfunctional kids, and how do you stop building them?"

A former high school teacher, the septuagenarian began taking students sailing in his family's boat more than 20 years ago.

"The growth, maturity and self-respect–not just the knot-tying and hoisting of sails–carry over to their lives," observes one teacher who has made the journey with these students.

As we steer our course through life, we need to remember the always-present love of God.

God is our refuge and strength, a very present help in trouble. Therefore we will not fear. (Psalm 46:1-2)

Guide me and guard me, Lord. Keep me safe today and always.

A Feast for the Soul (and the Body)

When hungry folks come to the soup kitchen at the Episcopal Church of the Holy Apostles in New York City, they are coming for more than the food.

Each Wednesday in the spring, the soup kitchen hosts a writer's workshop, encouraging the kitchen's homeless and poor guests to pour out their experiences and their souls on paper. More than 250 writers have participated in the program.

Many of the essays and poems produced through the workshop have been included in an aptly titled volume called *Food for the Soul*. The well-received book has garnered good reviews by major newspapers, because of the honest, sometimes painful, stories the writers have crafted about their lives on the street.

Every individual wants to be heard and has something worthwhile to say, regardless of the circumstances of his or her life. Give someone the loving gift of your rapt attention.

Listen and understand. (Matthew 15:10)

Spirit of Truth, help me shed my prejudices.

A Special Spring Break

College spring break may be best known for students going to sunny locations to enjoy themselves by partying.

Not Lauren Wisniewski. In her freshmen year at college she read about the Alternate Spring Break program, or ASB. It encourages students to spend their vacations helping others. Wisniewski and her friends from the University of Michigan spent their first spring break in Nashville helping Habitat for Humanity build affordable homes for less fortunate families.

Since that first spring break Wisniewski has become a leader in ASB. She helps organize groups of young adults who want to lend a hand on their vacation. She even sets up fundraisers to help pay the travel expenses of those who choose to give their time to help others. This means more to her then getting a tan.

Using your free time to help others is one of the most rewarding things you can do.

Help the poor. (Sirach 29:9)

Jesus, help young adults to spend their time and youth wisely, lovingly, in the service of the neediest.

Prayer on a Rainy Day

Often on weary, rainy cold days, we linger in the comfortable warmth of our homes and apartments. Some people, however, eat out of trash bins which later double as fire places. They sleep on the streets. These people often have nothing but the clothes they wear everyday and newspapers for insulation.

One afternoon, a young woman who was working her way through college sat next to a homeless man on a bus. Looking at the dreary sky he muttered, "Another night out in the rain."

As she walked down the bus aisle toward the exit the young woman prayed for sunny skies. Half an hour later God replied: the sun shone.

But, God also asks us to take action to remedy the scandal of homelessness. The human dignity and desperate need of our neighbors demands our efforts to serve those who have so little.

Because you trample on the poor and take from them...grain, you have built houses of hewn stone, but you shall not live in them. (Amos 5:11)

Imbue us Your own sense of justice and fairness, Just Judge.

Not So Perfect

If you're a perfectionist who drives yourself and those around you crazy in your efforts to do everything perfectly—or not at all—here's a suggestion: just do it.

While people should strive for excellence, no human being can ever be faultless. Mary Ann O'Roark, writing in *Guideposts*, says, "By telling yourself that you can do everything perfectly, you are, in effect, setting yourself up as God."

Instead, O'Roark believes you should "remind yourself that nothing you do will ever be perfect so there is no sense in holding yourself to impossible standards. You'll feel better about yourself once you realize that completing something is a worthy goal in itself."

Each of us has a worth and uniqueness in God's sight. Don't diminish it by seeking the impossible. Acknowledge your flaws. Commit yourself to fulfill God's plans for you—not impossible goals you set for yourself.

You are precious in My sight, and honored, and I love you...Do not fear, for I am with...everyone who is called by My name, whom I created for My glory, whom I formed and made.
(Isaiah 43:4,5,7)

Help me to trust Your plan for me, to put myself completely in your hands, Eternal God.

César Chávez: Hero

It wasn't always obvious that César Estrada Chávez would become a renowned labor leader, founder of the United Farm Workers and champion of the rights of migrant farm workers.

Chávez was born during the Great Depression, March 31, 1927. His parents, Librado Chávez and Juana Estrada lost their Yuma, Arizona, farm for non payment of property taxes. The Chávezes then became migrant farm workers in Arizona and California.

As a result, Chávez had a seventh-grade education and personal experiences of the racism and harsh working and housing conditions endured by farm workers and their families.

Chávez believed in non-violent protest, using hunger strikes, peaceful rallies and boycotts to achieve social justice for United Farm Workers' (UFW) members. He died in 1993 after improving the lives of countless others.

God expects us to work for justice and peace in our neighborhood, our nation, our world.

Wages are not reckoned as a gift but as something due. (Romans 4:4)

Workers are entitled to be treated fairly and with respect. Jesus, Carpenter, remind us that in seeking these rights for others we do so for ourselves.

Smile! You're in Church!

For too many, the idea of attending a weekly service is simply an obligation. Have you ever thought attending a religious service could be joyful, even fun?

A writer in *U. S. Catholic* magazine tells of attending a Mass in which a little boy, unable to contain himself, danced in the aisles, sang at the top of his lungs and generally had "a blast," as the writer described it. While a few members of the congregation tried to subdue the boy, the boy's parents believed that their son's joy was what church was all about.

"Let him enjoy it," said his dad.

Of course, religion includes the contemplation of serious issues, including life and death. Yet the Bible is filled with stories of people whose faith not only saved them from despair, but brought them joy. How can you extract more joy from your faith?

The prophet Miriam, Aaron's sister...and all the women went out...with tambourines and with dancing. And Miriam sang..."Sing to the Lord, for He has triumphed gloriously."
(Exodus 15:20-21)

I pray for a joyful spirit, Risen One.

Are You Being Called?

Ever feel as if you had another purpose in life? According to author Gregg Levoy, "Callings are intuitions, passions and voices that tell us how to find our true north."

How can you recognize your calling?

- Allow time for reflection. True callings tend to keep coming back. They have a power and persistence that is hard to ignore.
- Go with the flow. With a true calling the necessary mundane work isn't so onerous.
- Listen to your heart. "A true call is in line with your deepest values." Your calling...makes you feel more like the real you.
- Judge by the results. Do you feel energized by your new pursuit?
- Realize that you may get resistance from family and friends, as well as your own inner doubts.

Are you living the life you were meant to lead?

Stand at the crossroads, and look, and ask for the ancient paths, where the good way lies; and walk in it, and find rest for your souls. (Jeremiah 6:16)

Enlighten me as to Your will, Heavenly Father.

Travel in the Right Direction

How great is God's forgiveness? Rev. John Hampsch, C.M.F., author of *The Awesome Mercy of God*, reminds us that the word mercy is mentioned in the Bible more than 400 times.

And he offers hope to those desiring mercy: "If a traveler on earth were to travel east, he could do so endlessly without changing directions. The same would be true if he traveled west. But it would not be true if he chose to travel endlessly north or south" because a traveler who passes a pole would start traveling in the opposite direction because the earth's axis is north-south.

What has this to do with God's mercy? Our Creator is more unchangeable than the axis of the earth. And we have His promise: As far as the east is from the west, so far He removes our transgressions from us. (Psalm 103:12)

If we are overwhelmed by guilt, it's because we're going in the wrong direction.

My compassion grows warm and tender. I will not execute My fierce anger...for I am God and no mortal, the Holy One in your midst and I will not come in wrath. (Hosea 11:8-9)

Thank You, Almighty God, for Your unending mercy.

Unchaining Hearts

It took a while for Sherry Grace to speak up. But when she did, she helped to set a lot of mothers' hearts free.

For years the Orlando, Florida, mother kept silent about her two incarcerated sons. Then one day she decided to share her anguish with members of her church. Soon other mothers were approaching her, whispering: "My son is in prison too."

Realizing that others needed help, Grace founded "Mothers of Incarcerated Sons," which now assists 1,300 mothers of inmates in 23 states. The group has persuaded wardens to move inmates closer to their families and lobbied legislators to reexamine mandatory maximum sentencing guidelines.

Most importantly, Grace's organization helps mothers stop blaming themselves for what they did wrong as parents–and start focusing on a better future for their children, after prison. "Failure is temporary," says Grace.

Helping others, in ways big and small, always has a lasting effect.

Bear one another's burdens. (Galatians 6:2)

I place my trust in You, Compassionate Lord. Help me bear all my burdens.

Lend a Hand

A story is told about a statue of Jesus in a German cathedral that had had its arms blown off during World War II. Later, someone attached a sign: "Christ has no hands but yours."

Faith is something to be lived out and shared, notes *St. Anthony Messenger* columnist Susan Hines-Briggs. She has suggestions for ways our hands can do the work of Jesus.

For instance, we–perhaps joining with other family members or friends–can offer to paint a room, make repairs, clean a yard, shovel snow or shop for an elderly or ill neighbor.

It is easy enough to remain self-centered. We're busy. We have our own problems. "Sometimes we can use a good reminder that it's not all about us, and we are called to act in Jesus' name," writes Hines-Briggs.

Think about what you already do for others–and acknowledge your own efforts. Then ask yourself what else you can do today to touch another with loving-kindness.

A good measure, pressed down, shaken together, running over, will be put into your lap; for the measure you give will be the measure you get back. (Luke 6:38)

Help me appreciate what I do for others, Jesus. May this encourage me to show generosity with my hands and heart.

In God's Presence

The writings and conversations of a 17th-century monastic, Brother Lawrence of the Resurrection, born Nicolas Herman, have impressed many including the late author Rev. Henri Nouwen.

Nouwen says that Brother Lawrence's book *The Practice of the Presence of God* shows that "prayer is not saying prayers but a way of living in which all we do becomes prayer."

With the guidance of Brother Lawrence many 21st century people have learned to turn their attention to God every few minutes; to speak frankly and simply to God; to approach God with a childlike faith; to offer their work to God. They also make an effort to place their confidence in God; to try to make their heart a place of calm and silence; to try to treat others with kindness and to obey the Commandments.

"The soul—accustomed by this exercise to the practice of faith—can actually see and feel God," wrote Brother Lawrence.

O God, You are my God, I seek You, my soul thirsts for You; my flesh faints for You, as in a dry and weary land where there is no water. (Psalm 63:1)

Holy God, help me abide with You always and everywhere.

A Place of Paradox

Pilgrims might be surprised by the paradoxes they encounter at Jerusalem's Church of the Holy Sepulcher.

When writer Jerry Ryan visited the shabby and run-down church, he found the petty jealousies and animosities among the various Christian groups which share the church on display. With all the rivalries among Copts, Armenians, Latins and Greeks, he wondered if there was room for the Prince of Peace.

"It is one of the paradoxes of the Holy Sepulcher," says Ryan in *America* magazine, "that where Christian brokenness is put on display for all to see, there the profound unity of pious people of God is also manifested as nowhere else."

Ryan points out that believers don't ask, "whether those kneeling beside you are Catholic, Orthodox, Eastern Christian or Protestant. Here we are all united in a common faith and a common love, hoping to share in a common resurrection."

There is one body and one Spirit...one hope...one Lord, one faith, one baptism, one God and Father of all. (Ephesians 4:4,5-6)

Remind the members of Your scattered and divided church to respect each other's differences, Adored Redeemer.

A Labor of Love

We have a tendency to think that love involves only our emotions. In fact, love is a conscious choice to open ourselves to others; to care about and for others with our actions, not just our feelings. Here are some more ideas on love:

- "Love in dreams is easy, but love in reality is a harsh and dreadful thing." *—Fyodor Dostoyevsky*

- "Where there is no love, put love and you will find love." *—St. John of the Cross*

- "At the hour of death, when we come face to face with God, we are going to be judged on love; not on how much we have done, but on how much love we have put into our actions." *—Mother Teresa of Calcutta*

Love flows from person to person or it doesn't flow at all. More than that, true love for others, for ourselves, for God, is an achievement of grace and courage.

Love is strong as death, passion fierce as the grave...Many waters cannot quench love, neither can floods drown it. (Song of Solomon 8:6,7)

Spirit of Love, fill me with Yourself so that I may never fear to love with my whole heart.

Dream On

We've all heard the expression "pipe dream," meaning something that is unlikely to ever materialize.

Yet, many successful and happy people admit that it was their dreams–deemed too lofty, or unrealistic, by others–that kept them motivated on their path to success and fulfillment.

Michelle Madrid-Branch, a successful, Emmy-nominated anchorwoman, loved her job. Yet, "a voice inside kept saying that there was something else I was supposed to be doing." Soon, she realized her true profession–an advocate for adoption worldwide. "I was adopted, and I wanted to tell the world about my experience and help children-in-waiting find their own 'forever' families," she says.

Dreams can fuel great accomplishments and personal fulfillment. American naturalist and philosopher Henry David Thoreau said, "Dreams are the touchstones of our characters." Don't let naysayers calm the wind beneath your sails–dream on!

I will pour out My Spirit on all flesh; your sons and your daughters shall prophesy, your old men shall dream...young men shall see visions. (Joel 2:28)

May I remain ever growing into the person You made me to be, Loving God.

Cutting Edge Insects

A trip through the electronics store can seem like a visit to the cutting edge of technology: Every day, there are new products that seem like nothing we've ever seen before.

That's not always the case, though. For instance, the high-efficiency light emitting diode (LED), the technology used in state-of-the-art flat-screen computer monitors and plasma televisions, was first developed over 30 million years ago.

Physicists have found natural photonic crystals nearly identical to those developed in labs for LEDs in the wings of African swallowtail butterflies. The butterflies grow them much as we do fingernails or hair; the crystals are what create the butterflies' vibrant coloring.

The world is full of unexpected wonder. Where can you find it?

When Israel went out from Egypt...The sea looked and fled; Jordan turned back. The mountains skipped like rams, the hills like lambs. (Psalm 114:1,3-4)

Lord, help me to find the wonder in the world around me.

One Woman's Extraordinary Life

Tufts-educated pediatrician and Harvard-educated minister Rev. Dr. Gloria White-Hammond dreamed of missionary work in Africa soon after her marriage to the Rev. Dr. Ray Hammond, a Harvard-trained surgeon and minister.

But first, their daughters were born. Then they founded and co-pastored Bethel African Methodist Episcopal Church in Boston's Jamaica Plain. Still, Africa beckoned.

In 2001, White-Hammond traveled to Sudan to help redeem (at $33 each) the freedom of more than 2,000 women and girls taken as sexual slaves during that country's on-going civil war. Yet, she was forced to ask, "You bring them back to their communities, and then what?"

So she and a few other women organized "My Sister's Keeper" to help Sudanese women earn money which helps fund a village literacy program and a girls' school.

Physician, wife, mother, minister, missionary—facets of one woman's extraordinary life. Each life is extraordinary. How is yours?

Honor physicians...for the Lord created them; their gift of healing comes from the Most High. (Sirach 38:1-2)

Jesus, Son of Mary, help me recognize the extraordinary in life.

Giving Others a Break

Some young people believe that taking a break can mean giving a break to those in need.

For several years running LeMoyne College students have left the comforts of the U.S. to volunteer in the Commonwealth of Dominica, a poor and remote island in the Lesser Antilles.

Students get a variety of experiences from teaching in an elementary school to serving as big brother or sister, to visiting impoverished elderly residents. One group got the chance to help in the construction of a house for a homeless man.

Through these service projects LeMoyne College seeks to "help its students search for meaning and value, and to prepare them for leadership and service to promote a more just society."

How can you promote a more just society by your own actions and through the organizations you support?

It is well with those who...conduct their affairs with justice...they will be remembered forever. ...They have distributed freely, they have given to the poor. (Psalm 112:5,9)

Guide every aspect of my life that I may encourage peace and justice in our world, Holy Wisdom.

Trunks, Not Trucks

Elephants are apparently natural mimics.

According to zoologists at Tsavo National Park in Kenya, a herd of elephants there have been documented mimicking the sounds of trucks passing on a nearby highway. One of the elephants in particular has become so skilled at copying the sound of motors that it led a zoologist to comment in *National Geographic* magazine, "I was sometimes unable to distinguish between the distant truck and the elephant's calling."

There have also been reports of elephants mimicking frogs, other elephants and even humans humming. If true, they put elephants among the small number of animals that are capable of "vocal learning," a distinction previously credited only to humans, parrots and dolphins.

The world is full of wonders—sometimes we just have to listen a bit more closely to hear them.

The One who prepared the earth for all time filled it with four-footed creatures; the One who sends forth the light...This is our God. (Baruch 3:32,35)

Generous Creator, help me to appreciate the wonders of the world—Your world—around me.

What Children Need

Since we hear of so much violence against children, it would be wise to remember these "Commandments of a Child."

1. Don't expect perfection–my hands are tiny, my legs short.
2. Let me explore the world in security but without useless rules.
3. Patiently explain things to me.
4. Be sensitive to my needs, to what I resent.
5. Treat me as the gift I am: I am responsible for my actions, but give me good example.
6. Criticize what I do, but do not criticize me.
7. Let me make my own decisions and experience failure, so I can learn from my mistakes.
8. Don't compare me to others, especially my siblings, lest you destroy my self-confidence.
9. Don't be afraid to let me try some new things on my own.
10. Set me an example of prayer. Teach me to pray.

Train children in the right way, and when old, they will not stray. (Proverbs 22:6)

Imbue parents and children with mutual whole-souled respect and love, Loving Father.

Belief in the Power of Prayer

"There are many people who will call when they are in severe trouble and they appreciate being put on the prayer line," says Lucille Teresi who coordinates the prayer line for Christ the King church in Omaha. Teresi continues "When people really have tragedy or sickness...there's comfort and hope."

The pastor agrees. "It's a great people-to-people ministry," Rev. Steven Stillmunks says. "It's healthy spirituality to ask others to share prayers with you."

No matter the difficulty you or your loved ones face, reach out to others whether in church or synagogue, support group or prayer line, or one-on-one. You're sure to find people who want to help practically and prayerfully.

And don't neglect to pray for others as well.

I will give you my support. (2 Samuel 3:12)

Abba, teach us how to pray for each other as well as ourselves. Above all, help us draw closer to You day-by-day.

Offer Advice with Care

"Advice is not disliked because it is advice, but because so few people know how to give it," wrote 19th-century English essayist Leigh Hunt.

That's a good point. If you feel the need to offer advice, or even if you are asked for it, tread lightly. Rather than insisting that your way is right, simply offer suggestions.

Use expressions such as "I think" or "It seems to me" rather than give the impression that your view is the final word. Be graceful if your advice is not accepted. Concern for the other person's welfare is more important than proving that you're right.

In fact, this thought from scientist and statesman Francis Bacon is worth bearing in mind: "He that gives good advice builds with one hand; he that gives good counsel and example builds with both."

Good example is always a great teacher.

Let your gentleness be known to everyone. (Philippians 4:5)

It's often easier to tell others the right way to do things than to do it myself. Grant me wisdom coupled with humility, Spirit of Counsel.

Craving Comfort

According to a recent Cornell University study, both men and women crave comfort food– but different types, and for different reasons.

The study found that women tend to turn to sweets like cake or ice cream when they are feeling sad or lonely. Men tend to eat heartier foods, like steak or pasta, as a reward for accomplishment– as if they're trying to continue the good feelings they're currently experiencing.

Neither option is terribly healthy, and women have an added pitfall: In general, the study found, they tend to be more conscious of the calories they're consuming, and therefore feel even worse after they've binged.

Understanding why we do certain things can have a big impact on how we live. Take a look at your own habits and tendencies. What can you change to make yourself happier and healthier?

Apply your mind to instruction and your ear to words of knowledge. (Proverbs 23:12)

Divine Master, help me understand who I am and why I do what I do.

Changing Lanes on the Road of Life

Many of us can effect big changes in our lives by making small ones right now.

Take Joe Durand, a commuter who drives 35 miles to get to work. Sick of continually pumping the gas pedal, changing lanes and slamming on the brakes en route in an attempt to shave minutes off his lengthy commute, Joe made a small adjustment: "I found out that by maintaining a consistent speed, I was on the off-ramp at the same time as cars that had been speeding past me."

"Now, when I get to my desk, I feel calmer and more in control," he says.

Little changes can result in big improvements in the quality of life. Think small–it might make a real change for the better.

The kingdom of heaven is like a merchant in search of fine pearls; on finding one pearl of great value, he went and sold all that he had and bought it. (Matthew 13:45-46)

Help me be a positive presence in the life of just one person today, Holy God. And help me stay positive in my own life as well.

Getting Help from Yogurt

The historic Massachusetts home of former U.S. president John Adams and his wife Abigail Smith Adams needed help.

Years of sunlight and moisture had taken their toll on the more than 78,000 objects in the house at Adams National Historical Park. Rust-red wallpaper had faded to the color of a bad sunburn. Leather book bindings were cracked, and a filmy haze clouded gold-gild mirrors.

Coming to the rescue—the Colombosian family. The makers of Colombo yogurt pledged 20 cents to the park, up to $100,000, for every yogurt container lid mailed in by customers in a three-month period.

This is not the first time they helped preserve history. The corporation, now owned by General Mills, raised $50,000 for the Paul Revere House in Boston's North End.

Help can come from many sources. We need an open mind to recognize and encourage it.

Let us now sing the praises of...our ancestors... who made a name for themselves by their valor. (Sirach 44:1,3)

Our history is worth preserving, Rock of Ages. Show us how to balance the needs of the present and plans for the future with today's needs.

Leading through Actions

People may say that someone is a natural-born leader, but the reality is that at least some leadership qualities are learned.

And one of the best ways of learning comes from watching the good example of leaders we admire. Professional golfer Phil Mickelson remembers a lesson that the legendary Arnold Palmer taught years ago.

Mickelson and Palmer were at a tournament which, as usual, had a large number of behind-the-scenes volunteers. Palmer slipped away from the crowds and media to spend an hour signing autographs and talking with these volunteers. Mickelson quotes Palmer as saying, "I wanted to...let you know how much we appreciate what you do."

Palmer did more than express appreciation to the volunteers. He influenced a new generation of leaders in his field.

Pay attention to the good example you see–and be sure to show it to others, too.

Let us set an example. (Judith 8:24)

Open my eyes to the good that other people do and help me to learn from it and emulate it, Spirit of Counsel.

One Meeting, Two People

Most people know or have heard about Alcoholics Anonymous, or "AA," the voluntary, free and remarkably effective organization that helps those addicted to alcohol stay sober. Most believe AA was founded by Bill W., who failed in his own battle against alcohol addiction until he formed what is now known as the 12-step program.

The fact is, Bill W. didn't start AA alone. Hung-over and near the end of his rope, Bill W. agreed, at the urging of his wife, to meet with Dr. Bob S., a fellow alcoholic, to help each other into recovery. Their "15-minute meeting" lasted six hours. No one knows exactly what the two men discussed, but their dialogue set a pattern for future meetings.

Alcoholics Anonymous has been the path to sobriety for many millions of alcoholic people since 1935. And to think, it began with just two people talking.

Two are better than one, because...if they fall, one will lift up the other; but woe to one who is alone and falls and does not have another to help. (Ecclesiastes 4:9,10)

Blessed Trinity, don't let us forget that small efforts can lead to big changes for the better.

Better Living through Kindness

What's the secret to happiness? The great sages and philosophers have pondered this question for thousands of years. Albert Einstein, physicist, mathematician and scientist, came up with an answer that's as close to the truth as we can imagine: "Only a life lived for others is worth living."

Writer Jean Malouf agrees and believes that one can find true happiness by acts of kindness for others. She writes, "Kindness means empathy, true intimacy, encouragement, admiration, service, understanding, concern, truth, trust, and all that makes us true images of God."

Both donor and recipient benefit from kindness. Kindness can help transform the negative into the positive, the lonely into the connected, the despairing into the hopeful.

(Jesus) took her by the hand and said to her, "Talitha cum," which means "Little girl, get up!" And immediately the girl got up and began to walk about. (Mark 5:41-42)

Jesus, You embody kindness and compassion. Teach me Your love for others, that I might share it.

The Garden of Life

"It takes hard work to keep a garden thriving. But it's worth it," says writer Leigh Anne Jasheway-Bryant. "A beautiful garden not only feeds us and fills our senses, it also teaches us life lessons." In a *Family Circle* article, Jasheway-Bryant shares her insights about gardening and living.

■ Choose the attitude with which you welcome each day. It can be with happy expectation: "I can't wait to go outside and smell the roses" or dread: "I have to pull the weeds again."

■ A garden has plants that provide beauty, and others that provide sustenance. It's the same in life. No one does it all.

■ A garden needs extra care in times of stress.

Jasheway-Bryant concludes, "A garden is for sharing. Let the birds, the bees and your neighbors enjoy it. When you keep too much to yourself, you lose out on the joy that comes from giving."

The Lord God planted a garden in Eden. (Genesis 2:8)

Thank You for sharing Your garden, the Earth, with us, Creator. Inspire us to conserve it wisely.

Open the Pages to Learning

Many people treasure memories of being read to as children, and of reading to their own children.

That's why Ruth Goetzman of Colorado Springs, Colorado, volunteers for her church's "Birthday Books for Children" program. Church members and others buy new books in English and Spanish for homeless youngsters and bring them to shelters. From toddlers to teens, each child receives a hardcover book as a present on his or her birthday.

One day, Goetzman gave a book about learning to tie shoes to a three-year-old. The boy's father put the child on his lap, opened the book and said, "See? Now we can learn to tie your shoes!"

The volunteer said, "I could've stayed all day, watching them read together."

Help a child and you help the whole family. Extend your kindness to the young people around you.

My child, do not forget my teaching. (Proverbs 3:1)

Jesus, my Lord, show me how to imitate You in caring for those most in need of love.

Reaching the Summit

It took the better part of two decades, but Ed Viesturs made history when he became the first American to climb the 14 tallest mountains in the world.

Part of the reason his long-term quest to climb all of the world's 8,000-meter-or-higher peaks took so long was caused by a particular frustration along the way: Viesturs had to attempt Mount Annapurna, in Nepal, three times before reaching the summit. "Annapurna was the stumbling block," he notes, "and it took 16 years to get over it."

Still, Viesturs never gave up. "Once I start something, I don't like quitting until I'm finished with the project," he said.

The mountains you encounter in your own life may be more metaphorical than Viesturs' literal ones, but determination similar to his will likely help you surmount them.

Let us run with perseverance the race that is set before us. (Hebrews 12:1)

Everlasting God, help me to have the determination to climb the mountains that stand in my way.

The Family Business

There are three New York women who have several things in common. They all make the time to help others by volunteering. And, they are also all related.

Carol Geduldig has been an active member of her church for a long time. Her daughter Joyce Rivera serves as the program coordinator for the church men's shelter. Joyce's daughter Alicia Rivera has been volunteering there for six years.

They each have different reasons for helping. Alicia Rivera likes using her culinary skills to make special meals for the men in the shelter. Carol Geduldig enjoys getting out of the house and being useful to those in need. And Joyce Rivera sums up the main reason they choose to help out: "It's just a rewarding feeling knowing that you're helping people."

Handing down moral values and a volunteering spirit from generation to generation can help make the world a better place. How can your family do its part?

A woman who fears the Lord is to be praised....and let her works praise her in the city gates. (Proverbs 31:30,31)

Creator, bless women and girls with self-esteem, wisdom and generosity.

Finding Your True Calling

Like so many, Stephen Malkoff encountered a few detours on the way to finding his true calling.

As a youngster in Alabama, Malkoff loved trees. He'd climb the tall elms or oaks and feel the peaceful presence of God. "Sitting up there amid the swaying branches was almost like praying."

Malkoff studied architecture, but his real talent was elsewhere. "My buildings always ended up being attractive, but unbuildable," says Malkoff. "But my professors always liked the trees and plants that I'd put into my drawings to make the buildings look more realistic."

Although Malkoff switched to art, things really fell into place when he discovered his niche drawing trees. His work led to a commission to draw historically significant trees in every state. "When I'm drawing trees, I get that same feeling I got as a kid...trees bring me closer to God."

Find your true calling. You'll find yourself closer to God.

O Lord, how manifold are Your works! In wisdom You have made them all. (Psalm 104:24)

Blessed Father, help me find You in my paid work and in my household chores.

"We're lucky to have him..."

"Yes," Special Olympics coach Marcia Schneider told New Earth, the Fargo Catholic Diocesan newspaper, "We're lucky to have him. He's taught us way more than we've ever taught him."

Schneider was talking about her youngest son, Colten, who has Down syndrome. She adds that though it can be depressing to know that he is limited "he's the best thing that ever happened to us." She adds, "he really puts what is important in life into perspective."

Colten Schneider is blossoming in this loving atmosphere. There's peewee wrestling and second level swimming lessons; religious education; hunting and fishing with his father; and riding his bike. And since he is learning to read, 8-year-old Colten recently read in front of his first grade class for the first time.

A loving, accepting, supporting family is exactly what's needed for a boy like Colten; for any child with a disability; for sick children; indeed for every child and adult. Love promotes growth, blossoming, life.

Love one another deeply from the heart.
(1 Peter 1:22)

Cherish the parents of handicapped and sick children, Son of God.

Staying Tuned for Further Direction

It was April of 1994, and Maryknoll missionary Rev. Daniel Ohmann was listening to a report about war in the African countries of Rwanda and Burundi. At the time, he was in nearby Tanzania.

"The reporter asked a refugee what the people needed," Father Ohmann recalls. "The man's reply, 'Send us some priests.'"

And so Father Ohmann went to a part of western Tanzania four miles from Burundi; six from Rwanda. As many as 250,000 refugees a day were pouring into the area to escape the murderous warfare ravaging Burundi and Rwanda.

"I didn't see the violence itself, but I certainly saw its aftermath," explained the Catholic priest. "UN agencies (were) providing food and shelter, so we were able to devote most of our time to spiritual concerns."

The horror of warfare demands that we "tune in" to how we can be instruments of God's peace. Listen!

Sacrifice and offering You do not desire, but... an open ear. Burnt offering and sin offering You have not required. Then I said...I delight to do Your will, O my God. (Psalm 40:6-7)

Prince of Peace, hasten that day when wars shall have ceased and the world shall brim over with Your "shalom."

Finding God's Will

Even when we want to do God's will, it isn't always easy.

James Ingram grew up believing that he was called to be a minister. He entered a seminary and became a pastor in rural Virginia for twelve years. But he kept asking himself, "Is this where I'm supposed to be?"

So he became a business executive. Realizing this life was not for him, Ingram prayed, "Father, I promise to follow Your will in all I do." Returning to Virginia, he visited Colonial Williamsburg and finally found the right job. As an historical interpreter, his role is that of Gowan Pamphlet, a real slave in the mid 1700's, who became a minister and founded Williamsburg's first black Baptist church.

Says Ingram, "Here I am in the twenty-first century telling the story of preacher Gowan Pamphlet, and living my own, exactly where God meant me to be."

Seek God's will with your whole heart.

To obey is better than sacrifice, and to heed than the fat of rams. For rebellion is no less a sin than divination, and stubbornness is like iniquity and idolatry. (1 Samuel 15:22-23)

Lead me in the way of obedience to You, Your Will, Holy Lord.

Work: Just Part of Life

Some employers know that it's better for all concerned to recognize that employees have concerns outside the office.

One online real estate brokerage firm asks new employees to bring in photos of family and friends to be added to a montage at the entrance. "We realize that everyone has outside interests, friends, and family, and that maintaining a balanced life is very important," says the president.

When a hotel chain planned a recycling program, it made a point of explaining the community and environmental benefits to the maids who would do most of the work. They were glad to cooperate. "Doing the recycling is the most important part of my job and makes me feel like I did something important in the day," said one maid

Work is a key part of life, but it is only one part. Acknowledge, cultivate and celebrate the whole person you are.

Six days you shall labor and do all your work. But the seventh day is a sabbath to the Lord your God; you shall not do any work. (Exodus 20:9-10)

Jesus, Carpenter of Nazareth, remind me that who we are is more than what we do.

Older Women's Power

Women in what has been called the third age of a woman's life–well-past 50, never married women, widows and married women and grandmothers–are more and more discovering their power for peace and justice.

- Las madres de los desaparacidos, mostly mothers and grandmothers, have demonstrated regularly since the '70s for the return of loved ones "disappeared" during the Argentine military junta's 1976–1983 "dirty war."

- The 18 women, aged 59 to 91, some with walkers, one blind, another deaf, of the anti-Iraq war Granny Peace Brigade, tried to enlist with military recruiters in 2004. Arrested for disorderly conduct, the women were acquitted at their trial.

- In Nepal, 50,000 mostly illiterate mothers delivered measles vaccine to clinics. Then they went door to door publicizing vaccinations. Measles deaths dropped 90% in 2004.

Older women have a wisdom and a power that needs to be respected for the common good.

Speak out for those who cannot speak, for the right of all the destitute...judge righteously, defend the rights of the poor and needy. (Proverbs 31:8,9)

Cure society of age and gender bias, Lord.

When Someone Is Ill...

When a friend or relative has to cope with a serious disease or injury, we need to support them—and their primary caregiver—as much as we can. These suggestions may help you:

- Call before you visit. Stay alert to signs of fatigue, and keep visits short.
- Be sincere in what you say and avoid false cheeriness. A hug or a pat on the arm may be more meaningful.
- Send a note or card or call regularly, especially if the recovery is a long one.
- Treat the patient as a person, not an illness.
- Offer specific help to the patient and family, such as running errands, baby-sitting, giving a ride.

And pray for your suffering loved one, as well as the professionals, family and friends who are caring for him or her. Remember, God heals body, mind and spirit through His people.

Do not hesitate to visit the sick. (Sirach 7:35)

Divine Healer, touch Your suffering people and grant them wholeness and holiness.

Taping a Life Back Together

One night during the days when Tom Mullen was drinking too much, he ripped up all the poems he had penned—and passed out.

While he was sleeping it off, his wife taped together his writings and put it in a shoebox. More than 30 years later, when Mullen's wife died, he found that shoebox with the poems.

Life had turned around for Mullen in the years that followed that fateful night. And while finding the taped-together poems reminded him of those dark days, they also helped him remember his wife's great love—a love that had also pieced together his lost heart.

Even when life is in tatters and hope fades, the knowledge that one is loved by God and by one special person can restore hope and give us the strength to pick up the pieces and go on.

(Jesus) told them this parable: "Which one of you, having a hundred sheep and losing one of them, does not leave the ninety-nine in the wilderness and go after the one that is lost...When he has found it, he lays it on his shoulders and rejoices." (Luke 15:3-4,5)

Merciful Savior, please do not let me forget that You love me and will always search for me when I stray from You.

Day by Day by Day

When you find yourself overwhelmed by past problems or worries about the future, consider this principle championed by Dr. William Osler.

Osler, sometimes called the Father of Modern Medicine, was a celebrated Canadian physician and medical educator at the turn of the 20th century. He believed in "living for the day only, and for the day's work...in day-tight compartments."

He got the idea while on a ship. A warning bell sounded, and all the watertight compartments below deck were slammed shut. He realized that by shutting out other concerns or problems and focusing simply on the work of the day, it would eliminate "mental distress (and) worries about the future."

Osler suggested that we concentrate on what we can accomplish today rather than fretting about yesterday or tomorrow.

Trust God and live today, just today, as well as you can.

Look at the birds of the air...consider the lilies of the field...do not worry about tomorrow. (Matthew 6:26,28,34)

I often dwell on the past or fear the future. Lord Christ, take my burdens.

Baskets Full of Blessings

Theresa Wilson was devastated when her marriage ended. One of the things that helped her was the support of friends. She put all the notes and cards she received into a basket and frequently reread the kind words. "I started calling it my blessing basket," she said. "I always felt encouraged after I went through it."

In time, Wilson realized that a blessing basket could help not only the person who owned one, but also the person who made it. So she started a non-profit organization called The Blessing Basket Project. It purchases baskets from weavers in poor countries around the world which are then sold to buyers on-line and in certain retail stores.

"No matter how bad things are, always take time to count your blessings," says Wilson. "Gratitude can pull you out of even the deepest hole."

Take time to appreciate your blessings and to thank the Creator who gave them to you.

O give thanks to the God of heaven, for His steadfast love endures forever. (Psalm 136:26)

I have so much for which to be grateful, Generous Father. Enable me to grow in gratitude day by day.

Principles to Live By

Everyone needs encouragement. The periodical *Bits and Pieces* asked readers to write in with the encouraging words that direct their lives. Here are a few of those guiding principles:

Kathy Hague of Northwood, Ohio, wrote: "Use wisdom...if wisdom isn't enough use diplomacy...if diplomacy isn't enough use courage!

Robert Vera of Dorado, Puerto Rico, said: "A bridge uncrossed is like a life never lived, a door never opened, a gift never given, a love never shared."

And Bill Binder of Kinnelon, New Jersey, suggested: "It's not worth getting up in the morning if you can't learn something new by the time you get back in bed at night."

What words guide your life? Are they optimistic and heartening? Or do you stress the difficulties of life? Stay positive and you'll help yourself more than you could imagine.

The human body is a fleeting thing, but a virtuous name will never be blotted out. (Sirach 41:11)

Loving Friend, help me to speak to myself with enthusiasm and encouragement—and to speak to others with the same upbeat support.

Desperately Needed Heath Care

With their Harvard medical degrees and MacArthur "genius" awards, Paul Farmer and his colleague Jim Yong Kim could be doing anything. But the two physicians have chosen to help bring health care to poor and disadvantaged people.

In 1987, Drs. Farmer and Kim established a charity called Partners in Health in Boston. Well-equipped with all the components of modern medicine, it's a model for delivering public health services to poor people in Boston, as well as in Haiti, Russia, and Rwanda.

They solicit foundation grants, negotiate lower drug prices, train paid community health workers and provide hands-on treatment in clinics.

Dr. Farmer says, "I believe we can convince people that it's wrong for the destitute sick of the world to die unattended."

You may not be a physician, but you can help the destitute sick in your neighborhood, your state, your country and your world.

Come, you that are blessed by my Father, inherit the kingdom...I was thirsty and you gave me...drink...sick and you took care of me. (Matthew 25:34,35,36)

Divine Physician, remind us that we are responsible for one another, especially the destitute sick among us.

A Show of Appreciation

You have to like the positive attitude of the members of Appreciate New York.

"I want to appreciate you for who you are," Taz Tagore said as she approached a tired-looking New Yorker drinking coffee on a park bench.

She also handed a red appreciation button to a newsstand operator: "You provide us with snacks; you do such a good job." But he snapped impatiently: "I can't read English, my friend. Next, please!" and turned to a paying customer.

But as *The New York Times* story about the "volunteer appreciators" made clear, not everyone was aloof or rude. One street sweeper said it had been 17 years since anyone had expressed appreciation to him and the unexpected show of gratitude moved him to tears. Others smiled brightly or shared their own experiences.

Even if you don't have an "appreciation kit" with buttons, stickers and instructions, you can still find ways to let someone know they're not taken for granted.

The word of the Lord came to Zechariah, saying...show kindness and mercy to one another. (Zechariah 7:8,9)

Merciful Savior, remind us that most people are doing their best almost all the time.

On Biting Remarks

If more people knew the origins of the word *sarcasm*, chances are they would be less likely to be sarcastic.

The word itself comes from the Greek *sarcazo* meaning "to tear flesh." *The American Heritage Dictionary* gives these definitions of sarcasm: "A cutting, often ironic remark intended to wound; a form of wit that is marked by the use of sarcastic language and is intended to make its victim the butt of contempt or ridicule."

When we are aggravated or angry, we sometimes give way to sarcastic barbs at the expense of somebody else. Not only is this hurtful to the other person, it also diminishes us. So before we "tear flesh"–or the feelings–of another, let's make an effort to control any harsh words. More often than not, such wounds are slow to heal.

Gracious and gentle language will always do more good in the long run.

Pleasant speech multiplies friends. (Sirach 6:5)

Savior, guide my efforts to speak with as much kindness as wisdom.

How One Woman Aids Elders

Carolyn Reilly knows what it's like to be poor. She grew up in a federal housing project where she had two goals: to get out—and to help others. She did both.

She worked to put herself through college and law school. Eventually, she became the executive director of Elder Law and Advocacy in San Diego, a non-profit agency that provides free legal services to those over sixty.

They handled simple cases, but she wanted to take on fraudulent financial planners, contractors and others who scammed the elderly. Lacking the personnel or financial resources, Reilly wrote an editorial for the *San Diego Union-Tribune* about the legal problems of older people. Since then two law firms have supported her efforts by doing pro bono work.

"Be realistic in what you hope for," Reilly says. "Chances are you'll end up with more than you anticipated."

Persistence and perseverance can make all the difference.

Be persistent. (2 Timothy 4:2)

Open my eyes to see the problems of those around me, Holy Spirit. Then help me reach out to them.

And Now, a Word from the Experts

To many, motherhood seems like a constant journey or a work-in-progress for both the mother and her children.

Yet it's mothers themselves who are best equipped to advise on the challenges of motherhood. Here are some suggestions direct from moms:

- Because kids always want something when you're on the phone, tell them if they want an answer right now, it's "No." If they wait until you're off the phone, you'll consider it, says Shirley Derr.

- Allow your kids to get bored, says Monica Schardt. "It helps them cultivate imagination."

- Read aloud to your children every night, recommends McKey Berkman. "What we didn't anticipate was that this ritual would continue into high school," she says, delighted.

The most challenging jobs may hold the greatest potential reward. How do you view the difficulties in your life's work?

Those who respect their mother are like those who lay up treasure. (Sirach 3:4)

Thank You for the opportunity to serve others, Generous God—especially the next generation.

Making Mother's Day Special

Moshe and Ze'ev Forrest see Mother's Day not only as a day to honor and respect mothers. They also see it as a day to perform simple acts of kindness for bereaved strangers.

The Forrest brothers began delivering fragrant and colorful bouquets of flowers to grieving parents and children in South Florida since 2001, when their own father died of a brain tumor.

"I thought it would feel good, making someone else's day," says Moshe. "Someone whose child was no longer there to wish them a happy Mother's Day, or vice versa."

Said one benefactor of the brothers' efforts, "It's a simple act of kindness, but it helps ease someone's loss."

Losing a loved one is, without a doubt, one of the most difficult trials a person can endure. Seek to help the grieving. Often, the simplest efforts can lead to healing.

When the Lord saw her He had compassion for her and said to her, "Do not weep." Then He...touched the bier. (Luke 7:13,14)

Heavenly Father, have mercy on those grieving a loved one's death. Strengthen them, secure in Your compassionate, comforting love.

Family Traditions

When Bertha Cottrell Lee graduated from Wellesley College in 1910, she held on to the graduation robe she had purchased for the commencement ceremonies. In later years, to save money, each of her children wore the robe. The garment was also lent to other family members.

Ninety-five years later, Amanda, Bertha's great-granddaughter, wore the robe to her own graduation at Dickinson College. She was the 22nd member of the family to do so. The name of each of those people, along with their college and degree, has been sown into the lining of the gown.

"It definitely was a lot to bear, to have my family history on my back," said Amanda, "but it's a great feeling."

Family traditions bring people together and strengthen bonds between branches and generations. What traditions does your family hold?

I pray that...you may be strengthened in your inner being with power through His Spirit. (Ephesians 3:16)

Lord, thank You for gifts from my family and help me to share with them as well.

Sorry About That!

It seems there are two words in our language that are harder to utter for some than any others: I'm sorry!

Human beings sometimes go to great lengths to avoid saying "I'm sorry" even when they know they've hurt someone by their words or deeds.

One common response instead is to say, "I didn't mean it that way," or, "You took what I said (or did) wrong." Either way, such a response puts the blame on the person whose feelings were hurt. The offender skirts responsibility entirely.

It's important to own up to hurting another's feelings. Not that it's easy; it isn't. But such decisions do help define one's character.

Do you have the courage to say, "I'm sorry" when appropriate?

(The magistrates) came and apologized to them. (Acts 16:39)

Dear Jesus, fill me with the humility and courage necessary to take responsibility for my actions.

Canine Caring

While backing out of the hilly driveway from his California home, Michael Bosch's SUV flipped over and plunged 50 feet down a wooded slope. Trapped inside the overturned car, he sent Honey, his newly adopted dog and only passenger, through a hole in a broken window with instructions to "Go home."

But the cocker spaniel had a different idea. Honey ran to the nearest house and alerted a neighbor with her frantic behavior. In returning Honey to her home, the neighbor discovered Michael still trapped in his vehicle and immediately notified 9-1-1.

Home recovering from his injuries, Michael keeps Honey close to him realizing that if it weren't for the actions of his small friend he would not be alive.

We should all show appreciation to our four-legged friends. The loyalty of a pet makes a difference in our lives.

Better is a neighbor who is nearby than kindred who are far away. (Proverbs 27:10)

Thank You, God, for the pets who bring unconditional loyalty and love into our lives.

How to Grow in Prayer

Every one of us needs some encouragement from time to time in every part of our lives—including prayer.

Lawrence Cunningham, a professor of theology at the University of Notre Dame, offers these motivating ideas:

- Every attempt to pray is, at the same time, an act of faith. The very fact that we speak to God shows that we are reaching beyond ourselves.
- All attempts at prayer are good. Every effort to pray has its impulse in God's grace.
- Prayer is reciprocal. Even when God seems silent, He is with us. Watching and waiting are part of prayer.
- Prayer is a way of being. We can develop the habit of raising our hearts to God within the context of our daily lives.
- True prayer is given, not achieved. Everything comes from God as pure gift. Prayer, before it speaks is, above all, to listen.

Listen. Speak. Pray.

Daniel...continued to go to his house...and to get down on his knees three times a day to pray to his God and praise Him. (Daniel 6:10)

Spirit of Love, heal my yearning heart by filling it with Your grace.

A New Definition of Leadership

Meg Whitman is president and chief executive officer of eBay, one of the most successful enterprises in corporate America's history. Yet she has rebelled against the way corporate America manages its workers.

Whitman has created a radically more democratic corporate model in which the collective input of customers drives employees' actions and decisions. She works from a cubicle, not a corner office. She converses instead of commanding. She builds continual consensus. And earns trust through transparency. She believes people are basically good and hence trustworthy. Whitman encourages influence instead of power. "The key is in connecting with employees and customers in two-way communication," she says.

Respect for the unique worth and intelligence of each employee and each customer is revolutionary. Support managers and companies when they operate on the principle of respect.

Respect those who labor among you.
(1 Thessalonians 5:12)

Father, remind managers and employers—indeed, all those in positions of authority—that respect is basic to all relationships.

It's Never Too Late

Maintain your passion and curiosity about life. It's never too late to learn.

Marnell Jameson dreamt about learning "French and Italian while taking oil painting and harp lessons. But raising a family and having a career has been, well, a little time-consuming."

Nevertheless, she is finding that people of all ages are pursuing the dreams they had in youth as well as discovering new creative outlets in middle age and beyond.

One septuagenarian retired as a chemist and took up painting, saying, "I'd always loved art, but was never any good." Now her work, mostly pastels depicting Biblical symbolism, sell for hundreds of dollars.

"My dream is to learn to cook gourmet food and work as a caterer" says a San Marco, California, resident.

"My dream is to become a registered nurse," a Weirton, West Virginia resident says.

And your dream?

Nebuchadnezzar dreamed such dreams that his spirit was troubled and his sleep left him. (Daniel 2:1)

Bless our dreams, Gentle Jesus.

On Accomplishments–Small and Great

Few of us will be remembered long after we die, except by family and loved ones. Yet, that doesn't mean we don't contribute significantly to our neighbors' good or the world's welfare.

Here are a couple of quotes that remind us of the value of each person's accomplishments:

- "I long to accomplish a great and noble task, but it is my chief duty to accomplish humble tasks as though they were great and noble. The world is moved along, not only by the mighty shoves of its heroes, but also by the aggregate of the tiny pushes of each honest worker."   –Helen Keller

- "Few will have the greatness to bend history itself, but each of us can work to change a small portion of events, and in the total of all those acts will be written the history of this generation."
                                              –Robert F. Kennedy

Make your mark–change our world for the better.

Seek good and not evil. (Amos 5:14)

You have given me a task which belongs to no one else, Divine Master. Help me do my best today to fulfill it.

Finding Your God-Given Talent

Today, Alice Coles is recognized as a community leader in Bayview, Virginia. But there was a time when she didn't know how effective she could be.

In 1994, Coles joined her neighbors in opposing the planned construction by the state of a maximum-security prison. New to activism, Coles studied the issues and traveled to Richmond to testify. Her arguments were heard.

Bolstered by that victory, she went on to tackle the poor housing in her area. Many people lived in small shacks that lacked running water and heat. Faulty electrical wiring was a fire hazard. Coles organized her neighbors and started applying for and receiving federal and state housing grants.

"We have to look within ourselves for that one gift God has given us and use it," said Coles. "We just need to look around and see how we can make this world a better place to live."

You are the salt of the earth. ...You are the light of the world. (Matthew 5:13,14)

Inspire many to be doers and not only complainers, Jesus.

Psst...Have You Heard the Latest?

Gossip is an interesting phenomenon. People seem to love it, yet claim to feel guilty after gossiping. Some people rationalize their gossiping, calling it a "guilty pleasure."

Author Bob Burg, who wrote a book on the subject, sees it as much more. "Gossip is really defined as any kind of harmful or hurtful communication that's not absolutely necessary," he says.

Seen in that light, gossip doesn't seem so harmless, or appear to be a mere recreation used to pass the time.

Think again before engaging in gossip. Ask yourself whether or not the information is helping the person you're speaking or hearing about. If not, move on.

Whoever belittles another lacks sense, but an intelligent person remains silent. A gossip goes about telling secrets, but one who is trustworthy ...keeps a confidence. (Proverbs 11:12-13)

God, remind me that listening to gossip may contribute to others' hurt feelings or reveal confidential information.

Handmade with Love

Some ideas are so good that they accomplish far more than the person who came up with them ever imagined.

In 1996, Brigitte Weeks wrote an article for *Guideposts* magazine telling how she knit sweaters for refugee children and asking that others do the same. Ten years later, 300,000 sweaters have been distributed to youngsters from Appalachia to Uzbekistan.

Following a simple pattern provided by *Guideposts'* Knit for Kids project, volunteers work individually and in groups to provide warm, colorful sweaters along with the message that someone cares. Fay Hartline of Temperance, Michigan, says, "As I knit each sweater, I offer a prayer that God would hold in the palm of His hand the child wearing the sweater."

The next time you have a great idea to help people, share it with others. You never know just how much good you can do until you try.

Be ready for every good work. (Titus 3:1)

You have given me talents and abilities, Merciful Lord. Show me how to use them to benefit Your children.

Who Am I?

It's interesting how people can see us so differently. Is she "so nice, shy and gentle"? Or "stuck up"? Is he "an enthusiastic go-getter"? Or "too aggressive"?

For countless fans worldwide, Bob Dylan is a modern-day troubadour, a fantastic songwriter and the voice of a generation. For residents of Hibbing, Minnesota, Dylan is remembered as Bobby Zimmerman who left Hibbing and rarely returned. When asked, some remembered him as "a little weird" or "don't like his music." Others want to honor him for his contributions to music.

There will always be people who misunderstand you. And you're never going to please everyone. If you try you'll be "blowing in the wind" without a moral compass.

So don't worry so much about how others define you. Know yourself, your values. And, live accordingly.

Are not five sparrows sold for two pennies? Yet not one of them is forgotten in God's sight. ...Do not be afraid; you are of more value than many sparrows. (Luke 12:6,7)

Holy Wisdom, enable me to know myself and my values and to live them out courageously.

Stop Your Stress – Now!

Got a minute? Lessen your anxiety with these techniques:

- Stretch. Taking just 60 seconds to bend, twist and lengthen muscles can pulse needed oxygen to your brain and clarify your thoughts.
- E-mail or call a friend.
- Read something that makes you smile.
- Declutter your workspace.
- Take a deep breath – and slowly exhale.
- Make a list of your frustrations and fears. Read it; shred it!
- End a grudge, reconnect with a friend or work through a difficult issue with a spouse, sibling or child. You'll start to feel that stress slip away!
- Count your blessings.

Focusing on life's positives – and the fact that God loves you through the ups and the downs – can help you ease stress any time.

You are precious in My sight, and honored, and I love you...who (are) called by My name, whom I created for My glory, whom I formed and made. (Isaiah 43:4,7)

Slow me down, Lord, so that I may never miss Your presence; never fail to share Your love.

The Card that Led to a Sister—and a Law

In 2004, some five decades after Jeff Daly last saw his baby sister Molly, and after both their parents had died, the Oregon man found a small card in his dad's wallet with a Social Security number and the words "Molly Jo Daly."

More searching led Daly to the supervised group home where his developmentally disabled sister was living—and to the story Molly had in common with so many others who grew up in institutions in the 1950s. These children had had no connection to their families.

With pressure from Daly and his wife, the Oregon State Legislature enacted "Molly's Bill" in 2005 to make it easier for families to reconnect with relatives with developmental disabilities in state care.

In the meantime, Daly is making up for 50 years of lost time with his baby sister. It's never too late to reconnect with someone we love—or to right a wrong.

Love never ends. (1 Corinthians 13:8)

We are Your sons and daughters, Father, please forgive the wrong that we do.

Confessions of a Seven-Year-Old

Seven-year-old Hannah slept restlessly on the night before her first Confession. She knew all the steps for the Catholic sacrament of reconciliation, but her list of "sins" had her stumped.

"Mommy, what sins did you confess when you were my age?" Hannah asked as she was getting ready to go to church that Saturday. "How did you know what was a *real* sin?"

"Sometimes I told the priest that I was mean to my brother or my mother," Hannah's mom answered. "Other times I talked about not sticking up for someone when others picked on her."

"I think I get it," Hannah said, now seeming more relaxed. "Sin is when you don't love enough to do the right thing, or you forget about love and do the really wrong thing."

No matter our age, keeping up the love quotient in our day-to-day life will surely cut down on the possibilities of deliberately doing wrong.

'To love Him with all the heart, and with all the understanding, and with all the strength,' and 'to love one's neighbor as oneself,'—this is much more important than all whole burnt offerings and sacrifices. (Mark 12:33)

Pardon me, Merciful Savior, when I fail to love others as I love myself.

Have Goals Will Travel

"I never in a million years thought I would do a marathon, so now I feel like I could do anything," said Army Sgt. John Keith of Mississippi. after finishing the hand cycle race in the New York City Marathon.

"I really believe you've got to have goals when you're injured like this. I've seen people at the hospital who don't have goals, and they just sit there and slip away," he added."

Keith's left leg was amputated above the knee after a rocket-propelled grenade hit his Humvee in Iraq. The memory of two friends killed in that attack inspired him to stay in the race when he wanted to give up.

While recuperating at Walter Reed Army Medical Center, Keith had set three goals: get out of the wheelchair; move back home with his wife and children; finish the New York City Marathon.

His next goal? "I'd like to take my wife dancing."

Set important goals for yourself–especially hard ones.

Be strong and very courageous. (Joshua 1:7)

Compassionate God, help Your wounded people triumph over their grievous injuries as much as possible.

Secrets to a Longer Life

More and more people are living longer. In fact, by the year 2050, the United States will have an estimated ten million citizens aged 90 or over.

Dr. Claudia Kawas, a professor of neurobiology, neurology and behavior, believes people who far exceed average life expectancy have some things in common that have enabled them to live longer. What are they?

- Moderate daily consumption of caffeinated coffee
- A glass or two of wine most days
- Moderate body mass index–neither too plump nor too thin
- Physical activity
- Happiness
- Ability to accomplish daily living tasks independently

We can not guarantee ourselves a long, healthy life. But we can improve the quality of our lives and health. Begin today.

The days of our life are seventy years, or perhaps eighty, if we are strong...So teach us to count our days that we may gain a wise heart. (Psalm 90:10,12)

Holy Spirit, help me develop healthy habits of body, mind and soul.

Getting the Right Aisle Seat

Monica was emotionally shattered. She had just left her six-year-old Elizabeth crying hysterically in the car. Her husband and daughter had taken her to the airport for a business trip.

Knowing she would see little Elizabeth in just three "sleeps"–as she told her daughter–didn't give her much comfort as she boarded the plane. She found herself seated near a mom and daughter, Sue and Francesca. The child was six–just like Monica's Elizabeth.

During the flight, Francesca showed Monica a flower she made from a napkin. Monica mentioned that her daughter would have colored the white napkin with marker, saying that her daughter loved to draw and color.

As the flight landed, Francesca handed Monica her napkin-flower–complete with colors–saying, "I want you to have this."

Monica gratefully accepted, smiling inside at how sometimes–maybe with help from the angels–the sun shines while it rains.

The God and Father of our Lord Jesus Christ... consoles us...so that we may be able to console those who are in any affliction. (2 Corinthians 1:3,4)

Jesus, bring Your light into times of darkness.

Something for the Kids

Wesley Howard spent decades chasing children off his ancestral Jackson County, Oregon, farm, shotgun in hand. Generations of residents considered him the meanest man in the county. So when the life-long bachelor died of a stroke at age 87, there was shock at the reading of his will.

The putative "meanest man in Jackson County" had left his whole estate–valued at more than $11 million–to create a youth sports park on his 68-acre farm.

Jack Gundlach, one of the kids Howard chased away, said, "We always thought he didn't like kids." He added, "It changes everything. "It makes me think that maybe I shouldn't have been such a rotten kid."

Teach children to respect adults' privacy; to respect private property; to be kind to everyone. And be sure to show them good example through your own words and actions.

Do not speak evil against one another, brothers and sisters. (James 4:11)

Lord, give me wisdom and a share of Your patience and strength.

Bridges to Hope

When Han-Ya Hsu first arrived in California from Taiwan, she spoke no English–but she still understood the relentless teasing of her classmates.

Language was power, Hsu observed. She not only learned American English, but also went on to win academic awards and, in time, acceptance to Yale University.

Still, she never forgot her initial isolation. So in 2001, her sophomore year at Yale, Hsu started Bridges, a free English program for immigrants. Since then, more than 270 students from 35 countries have registered in the program.

"Bridges is not just about learning the language, but bridging the gap between cultures," explains Hsu. "Bridges offers immigrants a safe haven to express opinions and ask questions without anyone condemning or judging them."

Our own life's trials can make us stronger–and can push us to share that strength with others, offering them help and hope.

All of you, have unity of spirit, sympathy, love for one another, a tender heart and a humble mind. (1 Peter 3:8)

May my own life experiences enlarge my sympathy for others, Divine Master.

What Are You Passionate About?

You probably wouldn't be wrong to consider A. J. Jacobs a man obsessed. In his mid-30s, the *Esquire* magazine editor decided to read the entire *Encyclopaedia Britannica*. Thirty two volumes, each weighing four pounds; 33,000 pages; 65,000 articles; 24,000 illustrations; 44 million words.

His wife tried to distract him. "What about eating dinner at every restaurant in New York? You could start with the restaurants with A names and work your way to the Z's."

No, it was too late. Jacobs had his mind set.

From a cappella to Aaron to Antartica and on…so it went. Day in and day out. After one year and 55 days, Jacobs finally finished reading the encyclopedia. Then he turned his experience into a book he called *The Know-It-All*.

If you're like most people, reading an encyclopedia cover to cover might not interest you. Yet, finding a project or a cause that you're passionate about—now that is appealing. Live passionately!

I was zealous for the good. (Sirach 51:18)

Jesus, enable us to passionately, zestfully tackle the environmental and human problems of our age.

Show Children How to Help

Jonni McCoy was happy to take part in a yearly toy drive for children in homeless shelters. Yet she was uncomfortable reaching out to homeless adults on the streets.

But her youngsters wanted to know about these strangers–and how they could help them. So they prayed and came up with the idea for a "needs bag." They prepared bags with individual servings of non-perishable food, like tuna and crackers, pudding, juice and water, plus napkins and plastic utensils. Then they added inexpensive copies of the New Testament and lists of local services such as soup kitchens and shelters.

The McCoys keep several bags in the trunk of the car so they can stop, chat with a homeless person and offer the bag. They also pray for everyone they meet.

If you want to raise children of character who will mature into adults of courage and compassion, show them with your own actions.

Train children in the right way, and when old, they will not stray. (Proverbs 22:6)

Lead me in giving good example to others, Merciful Creator. And help me to learn by imitating the virtues of those around me.

Overwhelming Beauty

Michelangelo's statue of David, it seems, may be so beautiful that it actually disorients some people.

Dr. Graziella Magherini, a psychiatrist in Florence, has studied the reactions of visitors to David over the past 10 years. She's recorded responses that include increased perspiration, rapid heartbeat and dizziness. According to Magherini's study, 100 people have even needed to be rushed to the hospital.

Magherini attributes what she calls "David Syndrome" to the sensitivity of some tourists who are already tired and stressed. Regardless, she says, "We should not forget that a work of art is a very powerful stimulus."

There's beauty all around us in the world. Why not spend some time today looking for it?

From the greatness and beauty of created things comes a corresponding perception of their Creator. (Wisdom of Solomon 13:5)

Lord, help me to see the beauty with which You've surrounded me.

Booking Time for Reading

If reading barely makes it onto your family to-do list, it may be time for a change.

Reading-test scores in the U. S. have remained mostly flat for the last 20 years. Meanwhile in our information-driven society "an inability to read well can significantly reduce one's choices in life," according to Just Read Now, a Florida-based organization that promotes reading.

Solution?

- Designate a family reading time. Read anything and everything.
- Connect reading to bedtime. Let lights stay on for a while if your children are reading in bed.
- Take books or books-on-tape on family drives.
- Read to each other whatever and wherever you can, such as during a meal or while waiting in the grocery store line. And don't just read, but share understandings and interpretations.

The desire to read and the delight in doing so are among the greatest gifts you can give your children.

Give attention to the public reading of Scripture. (1 Timothy 4:13)

Holy God, help children and adults find joy in reading alone or to each other.

Your Job...Your Choice

Jane Boucher has empathy for people working at jobs they wish they could quit: "Stuck in a job that gets us down. You know the feeling. You dread Mondays. You watch the clock praying for the workday to be over."

Now a writer and public speaker, Boucher was once a high school counselor overwhelmed with too much paperwork and too little time to talk one-on-one to the students. She solved her problem and now shares what she has learned.

Before anyone quits a job, Boucher suggests making changes that will improve the situation. That might mean taking the first step to improve your relationships with your boss or with co-workers. See if your job lends itself to new learning experiences. One worker showed his superiors that by studying Spanish he could benefit the company.

But you also have to know when to say goodbye. Think things through, make the best decision you can–and act on it.

It is fitting to...find enjoyment in all the toil with which one toils. (Ecclesiastes 5:18)

Jesus, Carpenter, help the unemployed find work; those in dead-end jobs to find satisfaction; and those looking for new work to find meaningful employment.

How to Stop Smoking.

Just wanting to stop smoking is not enough. Experts advise getting help and making a plan for a smoke-free life.

According to *U.S. News & World Report,* "Researchers are learning more about how to improve your odds. ...Don't toss your butts right away. Smoking cessation experts say it's a bad idea to quit impulsively."

Even a few counseling sessions including "information, motivation, and tips" improve the chances of success. And new medications and nicotine gum, patches or nasal sprays also better your odds.

Psychologist Ricardo Munoz says, "You get the best quit rates when you give it everything you've got: psychological counseling, nicotine, and antidepressants".

Don't worry if you don't succeed at first. Every attempt increases the odds that when you do quit it will be for good.

Whatever habit you want to break or make–keep trying.

Happy are those who persevere. (Daniel 12:12)

Faithful Lord, help us establish good health habits and quit bad ones—for our own sakes and for our loved ones, too.

Building Up a Neighborhood

Kathy Henderson found the perfect home for herself and her daughter in Washington, D.C.'s Carver Terrace region.

Unfortunately, the neighborhood was a nightmare. Henderson's dream home was surrounded by gunfire, drug markets and crack houses. She turned to the local police, but got little help and realized that she had to take matters into her own hands.

With the assistance of other concerned community members, Kathy Henderson was appointed "neighborhood commissioner" and organized the Orange Hat Patrol—a citizen-watch group. She made it clear to the drug dealers that she would not back down. Her actions put pressure on the local police, forcing them to work with her to help clean up the area's crime.

Now, the neighborhood "is not perfect, but it's far better," says Henderson.

Pray for the courage not to back down, to do what's right even in difficult or dangerous situations.

Be courageous and valiant. (2 Samuel 13:28)

Inspire people to fight for welfare of their neighborhoods, Eternal Father.

A Resort for All to Enjoy

Disabled travelers know that, except for some cruise ships and designated rooms at certain large resorts, their choices for vacations are rather limited.

But the options are broadening thanks to Stanley Selengut, an ecotourism pioneer. When he started to lose his vision to macular degeneration, he revamped plans for his newest eco-resort, Estate Concordia, on St. John in the Virgin Islands. Special ramps and railings, extra-wide bathrooms, easy to use fixtures and appliances help people in wheelchairs and others to enjoy the facilities. Selengut also worked with local merchants to make the beaches as well as taxis and small boats more accessible.

Ileana Rodriguez, a 19-year-old paraplegic from Miami, said, "I never thought I'd have this kind of vacation."

Because one man didn't let his own problems defeat him, others will benefit. Whatever your situation, do your best to help others as well as yourself.

Rejoice in hope; be patient in suffering. (Romans 12:12)

Please don't let me be overwhelmed by my own difficulties, Merciful God. Show me how to keep lighting candles of hope for those around me.

The Mistakes We Make

Nobody can keep from making any mistakes, but some are more harmful than others. William Arthur Ward, author of several books, including *Thoughts of a Christian Optimist,* suggests that, as much as possible, we avoid these mistakes:

- Remorse over yesterday's failures.
- Anxiety over today's problems.
- Worry over tomorrow's uncertainty.
- Waste of the moment's opportunity.
- Procrastination with one's present duty.
- Resentment of another's success.
- Criticism of a neighbor's imperfection.
- Impatience with youth's immaturity.
- Unbelief in God's providence.

We need to forgive ourselves, our flaws and failures, just as God wants us to forgive others—and to keep trying our best each day that God grants us.

Forgive us our debts, as we also have forgiven our debtors. (Matthew 6:12)

Guide me, Holy Spirit, with Your wisdom and counsel, in the choices I make this day and everyday.

One Bright Idea

For women tired of rummaging around their handbags to find keys or other items, help is in sight.

A prototype for a solar-powered bag that automatically lights up when unzipped is being patented. The inventor? Rosanna Kilfedder, a 24-year-old design student from Scotland, who had noticed how often friends used the light from cell phones to search their bags.

Called the "Sun Trap," its inventor also thought "about safety and usefulness, and had the idea of including a portable charger for emergency situations." That means cell phones and PDAs can get a brief charge. The system is also flexible. Kilfedder says that it can be fitted into any bag with a zipper.

Creativity is more than having a great idea. It means being open to possibilities and potential around us. Whether you want to invent a successful product or solve a nagging problem, keep your thinking fresh—and consider the needs of others.

The wisdom from above is first pure, then peaceable, gentle, willing to yield, full of mercy and good fruits, without a trace of partiality or hypocrisy. (James 3:17)

Help me solve problems by using the ingenuity and intelligence You have given me, Creator.

Shy and Not Retiring

If you feel your shyness is a burden or barrier to an active life with rewarding relationships, consider the following.

"New research reveals shyness to be a valuable trait that can provide greater social sensitivity, self-reflection and a heightened ability to relate to others," according to Alexander Avila in *Catholic Digest*.

The author identifies seven strengths of shy people: sensitivity, listening, modesty, mystery, gentleness, reflection and loyalty. People who are kind and care about others make treasured companions. People who spend time in deep thought often solve complex problems. Good listeners are widely valued.

Among the shy notables Avila mentions are Mother Teresa of Calcutta, Albert Einstein, Princess Diana and Rev. Dr. Martin Luther King, Jr.

If you're shy, you're in good company and you can *be* good company, too. Recognize your special strengths and put them to good use.

Learn from Me; for I am gentle and humble in heart. (Matthew 11:29)

Jesus, help me to value my own unique person-ality and others'.

When Marriage Makes You Sick

If slamming doors and sharp words are the foundation of your couple-communicating skills, now hear this: A bad marriage is bad for your health!

A recent study by husband and wife researchers Ronald Glaser and Janice Kiecolt-Glaser at Ohio State University indicates that spouses in hostile relationships have consistently elevated stress levels that significantly impede their bodies' wound-healing capacity.

"If they're chronically contentious or difficult, there's a clear toll on the body," explains Kiecolt-Glaser, emphasizing that in the study the "quality of the relationship is the issue."

"We didn't look at people who were 'just having a bad day,' and so we saw that there is a clear physiological cost to chronic bickering that could have negative long-term consequences," she says.

All of this proves that in marriage as in life choosing to be people of peace and love is good for both body and soul.

So far as it depends on you, live peaceably with all. (Romans 12:18)

Lord, in our struggles, let us rejoice that You are near to help us.

Something in Common

Lt. Col. Rick Bowyer and his men were on a mission to find and rebuild the Hiba Institute, the only school in Baghdad for children with Down Syndrome. It was a meaningful assignment for the 41-year-old Kansan because he and his wife have a young son with Down syndrome.

Sahira Mustafa and her husband Hashim Monsour ran the school using their own money and private donations, naming it for their 23-year-old daughter, Hiba, who has Down syndrome. But their funds were running out.

"Maybe this is why the Lord placed me here," thought Bowyer who was able to provide the school with relief funds and supplies from the U. S. to keep it going. Someday, he hopes to be able to bring his son Sam to Iraq to visit the school.

We all have opportunities—and obligations—to do what is right and just for both friends and strangers.

Act with justice and righteousness...do no wrong or violence to the alien, the orphan, and the widow, or shed innocent blood. (Jeremiah 22:3)

Teach all nations to value and work for justice and peace for every one of Your children, Just Judge.

A Decades-Old Apology

In a speech on ethics in journalism, John S. Carroll, editor of *The Los Angeles Times,* suggested that the Lexington, Kentucky *The Herald-Leader,* which he once edited, carry this "clarification": "It has come to the editor's attention that *The Herald* neglected to cover the civil rights movement. We regret the omission."

Current editor John Voskuhl accepted the challenge, publishing a front-page exposé, two sidebar articles and a full page of previously unpublished black-and-white photographs describing how the newspaper had ignored the civil rights movement.

The omission had been a conscious strategy by former managers "to play down the movement" in hopes that it would wither away. "I would say better late than never," said the Rev. Henry W. Jones who participated in many sit-ins.

It's never too late to right a wrong; to say, "I'm sorry;" to acknowledge injustice.

In passing judgment on another you condemn yourself. (Romans 2:1)

Forgive us Creator, for judging Your children, our brothers and sisters by the shade of their skin, their ethnic or national origin or their religion.

Raising Moral Children

A recent headline read, "Raising moral kids in an immoral world." Actually, it's the actions and decisions of we human beings that are immoral or moral.

For example, a woman and her son heard a radio news flash about a celebrity's indictment on child molestation charges. The boy, visibly upset, asked his mother, "Why would a grown man want to do that?"

Drs. T.B. Brazelton and Joshua Sparrow, coauthors of *Mastering Anger and Aggression* say that parents should help children understand values and turn such moments into opportunities to teach morality.

- Set and communicate clear limits on behavior. Limits, say Brazelton and Sparrow, tell children, "I care enough about you to tell you what you need to hear, even if it upsets you."

- Emphasize that all actions have consequences. The authors believe "parents can give their children the clear message that doing the right thing is central to their family's identity."

The Lord honors a father above his children, and He confirms a mother's right over her children. (Sirach 3:2)

Abba, bless parents with prudence when guiding their children's moral development.

A Desperate Plea, an Honored Promise

Ryan Nielson knew it was his son's voice on the other end of the phone, but the message seemed unreal, impossible.

"Dad," said the distraught teen, "I was arrested for driving under the influence of alcohol ...I hit a pedestrian...and I don't think she's going to make it."

Devastated, Nielson began pleading with God. "Please, let the girl live. I'll make it up to You," he prayed.

Thankfully, the girl survived. Nielson kept his promise, and launched Designated Driver 4U, a Salt Lake City-based volunteer operation that offers free rides home to anyone who's had too much to drink.

"We make sure people get home safe, and others do too," says Nielson.

Some mistakes cannot be undone. Others offer the opportunity to ask forgiveness and to make amends.

All of us make many mistakes. (James 3:2)

May we each find the strength, wisdom and perseverance to right our wrongs, Lord.

What Would You Do for Love?

A magazine asked its readers: "What's the craziest thing you ever did for love?" The responses were warm and wonderful; even a bit wild and wacky. Here are a few:

- My husband and I spent a month in Kazakhstan adopting our daughter...a country I had barely heard of a year earlier. She was worth every second."

- "In college I took skydiving lessons and jumped out of an airplane to impress a new boyfriend..."

- "The craziest thing I've done for love was never walking away over the first five years of my marriage."

- "It was my husband who did a crazy thing for love. When I was having chemotherapy for breast cancer, my husband shaved his head. ...It made my baldness seem more normal during a very abnormal time in my life."

Allow love into your life, keep love in your life, and do something wonderful.

Love is strong as death, passion fierce as the grave. (Song of Solomon 8:6)

Remind us, Holy Wisdom, that while love is neither easy nor effortless, it is wonderful and life-giving.

A Parent's Love

Greg Grunberg, who played a CIA agent on the TV show *Alias*, had to contend with a difficult turn in the life of his son Jake when the child was diagnosed with pediatric epilepsy.

Despite his personal fears and worries, he realized that he needed to help other children and their families. Grunberg signed on fellow celebrities to create original finger paintings that were then auctioned off and sold as greeting cards. As a result, Grunberg assembled more than 100 paintings and has helped raise $350,000 for the Pediatric Epilepsy Project.

Although Jake is doing well on his medication, Grunberg hopes to raise enough research money to someday find a cure.

When illness hits someone we love, especially a child, it's not uncommon to ask why. Yet, if we search for creative solutions and share our resources, however modest, we can make a difference for the better.

He cured many who were sick with various diseases. (Mark 1:34)

Inspire our efforts on behalf of causes closest to our hearts, Creator of all that is.

Success's Sweet Smell

Until recently, the sense of smell was a mystery. But that changed through the scientific efforts of Linda Buck and Richard Axel. For their work, they were awarded the 2004 Nobel Prize in Physiology/Medicine.

"We discovered that the odorous chemicals in the air are detected by 'odorant receptors,' which are proteins in the nose," says Buck who works at the Fred Hutchinson Cancer Research Center in Seattle. "In the same way that letters of the alphabet are used to form written words, these receptors are used in varying combinations to identify different chemicals." These coded signals then go to the brain for translation: "Gasoline has a different code from roses."

The accomplishments of these scientists and others contribute much to the sum of human knowledge. Be grateful for all who in any field strive to learn the truth and to share it.

An intelligent mind acquires knowledge. (Proverbs 18:15)

Thank You, Spirit of Knowledge, for inspiring women and men to pursue Your truth in any and all ways.

The Bicycle Doctor

Since 1997, retired mechanical engineering professor Richard Klein has taught over 800 disabled or challenged children how to ride a bicycle.

Klein spent most of his 30-year career studying how bikes work, and has designed a series of special bicycles that give a new perspective on life to special-needs children. He and his wife Marjorie run over a dozen "bike camps" annually across the country.

Known to many as the "Bicycle Doctor," his work helps youngsters to build self-esteem, and challenges their "I can't" attitude by saying "You can."

He says, "When you teach a child to ride a bicycle, you put a piece of magic in them...and wonderful things happen."

We can each use our own "magic" to help those who can not help themselves.

Help the weak. (1 Thessalonians 5:14)

Remind us, Merciful Savior, that in helping others we help ourselves to grow more like You—kind, patient, generous.

Honoring Special Achievement

Who inspires you? Once a year, *Women's Day* magazine honors women whose special achievements inspire others.

Lydia Floyd founded Hands For Hope in California, a free after-school program. Youngsters learn about cooking, drawing, financing and sport. Most importantly, they get help with homework. Floyd says, that "It's ...important to expose kids early to a variety of things, to open their eyes to the wider world."

Oklahoman Carolyn Craven founded and directs Families Helping Families, a food and clothing bank. She "learned that you can't always tell who is hungry by the car they drive or the clothes they wear."

Lisbeth Riis Cooper and her husband, Don, found a way to assist people like their daughter with serious mental illness. They raised funds and began a healing farm community for the mentally ill in North Carolina.

"Who inspires you?' is a good question. "How do you inspire others?" is another.

The good person out of the good treasure of the heart produces good. (Luke 6:45)

How can I make a difference for a person or group of people, Redeemer?

The White Giraffe

Researcher Charles Foley first heard stories about a white giraffe in 1993, when he began working in Tarangire National Park in Tanzania. He spent years trying to track it down.

"Despite intensive searching, I never saw the giraffe," he recalled. "Sightings stopped coming in, so I assumed it had died...I never stopped looking, though."

In 2005, his quest ended—while conducting an aerial survey, a distant white reflection caught his eye. "I looked...blinked...and it was still there," he said. It was a white giraffe.

Foley took photos of the animal, which he conjectures is the product of leucistism, an albinism in which pigment is not totally absent. While there's no way to tell if it's the same giraffe he first heard about, he's satisfied that he's fulfilled his quest.

Goals may not always be easy to attain, but keep at them—you never know when you might fulfill your ambitions.

Endurance produces character. (Romans 5:4)

Blessed Trinity, give me the resolve to keep trying to achieve my goals—and Yours.

Lending an Ear

Mark and Christine had been through one trial after another. Serious medical concerns and financial stress finally forced the California couple to declare bankruptcy.

Then Ed McElmeel visited. Representing Stephen Ministries, he brought no money or medical advice, but only a shoulder to lean on, an ear to listen, and an open heart.

"We'd sit and talk," Mark says, "sometimes about very little–and sometimes about deep things."

Stephen Ministries, founded in 1975 in St. Louis by a Lutheran pastor, is named for Christianity's first deacon, who cared for the needy in the earliest Christian community. To date Stephen Ministries has trained more than 300,000 ministers to be there for people in hard times.

Sometimes it's not so much what we do for people–it's just that we are there for them.

They chose Stephen, a man full of faith and the Holy Spirit, together with (others). (Acts 6:5)

Loving Lord, may I bring Your light to all.

Reduce, Reuse, Recycle

Michael Sullivan, director of education for the Phoenix-based organization Take Charge America, offers the following warm weather energy saving ideas:

1. If the air-conditioning is on, close windows and doors.

2. Monitor water usage indoors (take showers not baths) and out (limit watering the lawn or washing walkways).

3. Wash only full loads of laundry and air dry.

4. Enjoy the sunshine; keep lights off as much as possible.

5. Reduce gasoline consumption.

These are just a few suggestions. You can probably come up with even more energy-saving ideas, and not just ones for warm weather. Challenge yourself and your family to begin practicing a new idea each month.

Protecting earth's limited resources is everyone's responsibility.

It is required of stewards that they be found trustworthy. (1 Corinthians 4:2)

Remind us, Creator, that we are responsible to each other and to You for our stewardship of earth's scarce resources.

The World's Children in Danger

The statistics are heartbreaking, shocking and shameful. Millions of children worldwide suffer from malnutrition and disease; they are trafficked; and they are exploited economically and socially in other ways according to an annual report issued by a Vatican agency.

In many cases, the stage is set for abuse because the children's births aren't registered. Children work under hazardous conditions operating dangerous machines, handling toxic materials or spending hours in poorly ventilated mines. Many are forced into prostitution or conscripted into armed conflicts.

"They are the scandal of our time," states the report. "For 860 million children of the world, the future is an unknown and the present is a nightmare."

If you saw the youngsters in your family and neighborhood being harmed, surely you would act. Can you do less for the children you don't know?

It would be better for you if a millstone were hung around your neck and you were thrown into the sea than for you to cause one of these little ones to stumble. (Luke 17:2)

Jesus, how can we protect children from harm?

Doing Good—One Copy at a Time

The next time you need computer or printer supplies check with some monks.

In 2002, Rev. Bernard McCoy of the Cistercian Abbey of Our Lady of Spring Bank in Wisconsin started a for-profit organization selling discounted toner, printer cartridges and other items to support the Abbey. The first year LaserMonks.com earned $2,000. Three years later, they made $2.5 million.

They put the funds to good use by contributing to dozens of charities around the world—from a Minnesota camp for children with HIV to a Buddhist orphanage in Tibet.

The self-supporting, cloistered monks who follow the Rule of St. Benedict, depend on media coverage, word-of-mouth and Rev. McCoy's speaking engagements to spread their story.

Everyone has a unique opportunity to serve God and His people. Don't be afraid to try something different in the service of others.

O God of my ancestors and Lord of mercy...give me the wisdom that sits by Your throne. (Wisdom of Solomon 9:1,4)

Holy Spirit, guide me in seeking the welfare of my brothers and sisters as well as my own.

Preparing for the Worst

Worries about terrorism, natural disasters, fires or other events may cause us to ask how we can be prepared if we must evacuate our homes.

Joseph Hearn, author of *If Something Happens to Me,* advises that each household prepare a grab-and-go case with important legal, financial and insurance documents. Include birth certificates, wills, Social Security cards, passports, plus copies of all drivers' licenses. Be sure to include lists of prescriptions, computer user names and passwords, bank accounts and credit card numbers, as well as emergency cash.

As a backup, Hearn advises keeping copies of important records in a safe-deposit box or with a trusted friend or relative.

We all have the responsibility to make plans for our own safety and that of our loved ones. A little foresight and preparation makes a big difference in rebounding from a difficult time.

I trust in You, O Lord; I say, "You are my God." My times are in Your hand; deliver me...save me in Your steadfast love. (Psalm 31:14-15,16)

Spirit of Counsel, enlighten me on how to look after myself and my loved ones, even as I trust myself to Your care.

Play It Again...and Again...

Do you love your work?

It's true that every job includes tasks that are boring or even unpleasant. However, people who really love their work are willing to take care of those small, everyday details that are necessary to achieve their goals.

The great Jazz musician Benny Goodman was practicing his clarinet one day near an open window. He saw his wife working in the garden. Later, she asked him how he could bear to keep repeating the same task over and over. He replied that he had been thinking the exact same thing about her.

Afterwards, Goodman said that he believed that "good results depend inevitably on the work one is willing to put into it. In the work itself—whether planting or practicing—you find your true enjoyment."

As much as you can, try to do work that gives you true enjoyment.

Commit your work to the Lord. (Proverbs 16:3)

Heavenly Father, help me work with zest and patience, for my good, the good of my neighbors, and Your glory, so that all I do will be for Your glory.

An Act of Love

Shortly before writer Ann Hood and her husband left for China to adopt their baby daughter Annabelle, her friend Mary called.

Mary invited her to dinner. At the restaurant, Hood recognized several other friends. She was confused at the apparent coincidence because she didn't think they knew one another. Actually, it turned out that all of the women at the restaurant that night had knitting in common.

As Hood puts it, "these friends, these women had secretly been meeting for six months, ever since they had seen the picture of our baby. They had knit (Annabelle) a blanket." That night they presented Ann with their precious gift.

"How blessed I was to have these friends …and what a blessing that they'd found one another! A baby 6,000 miles away had brought them together."

Rejoice in the gift of friendship!

Faithful friends are beyond price; no amount can balance their worth. (Sirach 6:15)

Inspire couples who can not have children to adopt children in need of a family, Lord of life and of love.

Volunteering Can Increase Your Happiness

Did you know that volunteering to help others can actually make you a happier person?

According to Dr. Ruth Peters, a frequent contributor to NBC's popular *Today* show, a compassionate person is a happy person. This also applies to families, says Dr. Peters. She adds that parents can follow concrete yet simple steps to instill greater compassion—and happiness—in their children.

"Empathy is one of the most teachable of emotions—but your child must be given the opportunity to learn it," she says.

Dr. Peters emphasizes that parents should set a good example by making volunteering a priority. "Volunteer with kids, donate family time and perhaps a bit of your own resources," she recommends. "Discuss, teach and live gratitude, and so will your children."

The result? Happier people, enlivened by the joy of giving.

It is well with those who deal generously. (Psalm 112:5)

Jesus, inspire families to volunteer together for worthwhile causes.

Change Your Thinking about Change

Benjamin Franklin was always trying to make things better. He was 79 when he wrote of his "bold and arduous project of arriving at moral perfection."

If you want to improve yourself (and who among us doesn't?) there are a few things to keep in mind.

First, appreciate that lasting change is a difficult, though not impossible, process. Then...

- Be certain you're ready for the change.
- Set realistic goals.
- Establish a system of rewards.
- Seek support.
- Substitute a healthy habit.
- Don't give up.

Franklin, of course, never reached perfection, but as he wrote, "I was by the endeavor, a better and a happier man."

"If you wish to enter into life, keep the Commandments." (Matthew 19:17)

Savior, keeping the Commandments requires life-long effort. Strengthen me with Your grace so I can make the attempt every day.

Bringing God to the Bargaining Table

When Jerry Butkiewicz was growing up, he and his siblings painted houses with their dad for much-needed extra family income.

His parents' sacrifices pushed him to help today's families make ends meet without working extra jobs.

Butkiewicz heads the San Diego-Imperial Counties Labor Council, an association of labor unions representing more than 100,000 working families in Southern California. For him, faith, family values and the rights of workers are connected.

"We need to fight to give people a job with a salary they can live on, health insurance, and dignity on the job," Butkiewicz explains, speaking of the principles that guide him when he's seated at the bargaining table.

As we ask God to bless the work of our hands, we should make sure that our daily labors are done to praise and thank Him and for others' good.

Let the favor of the Lord our God be upon us, and prosper for us the work of our hands. (Psalm 90:17)

Father, in all I do this day, may my actions give You praise.

The United States' Birthday

On anniversaries we remember and reflect upon the event. And so it is today, on the United States' birthday, that we think about The Declaration of Independence. The foundational document for that ongoing bold political experiment which is the United States, the Declaration says that:

"All men are created equal, that they are endowed by their Creator with certain unalienable Rights, that among these are Life, Liberty and the pursuit of Happiness. That to secure these rights Governments are instituted...deriving their just powers from the consent of the governed.

Unfulfilled, unrealistic or impossible ideals you say? Imagine your life without them. Then do all in your power to see to it that our nation reaches for these goals daily.

What does the Lord require of you, but to do justice, and to love kindness, and to walk humbly with your God? (Micah 6:8)

Like our founders, God, give us the courage to pledge "our lives, our fortunes and our sacred honor" to that bold experiment which is the United States.

Cell Phones: Progress or Impediment?

Because of mass appeal, easy accessibility and ever more affordable prices, cell phones – and the mass use of them – are here to stay.

There are individuals who are not buying into the cell-phone craze, however. Take writer Robert J. Samuelson. In a *Newsweek* magazine article he declared that he was becoming "the last man in American without a cell phone."

Why? Samuelson believes cell phones can be dangerous because they distract automobile drivers and lead to accidents. More than that, he believes that they interrupt people during their leisure time, blurring the separation between work and play.

Finally, he objects to the fact that cell phones have allowed private conversations to become public, contributing to a decline in overall common courtesy.

Just because something is popular and widely accepted, doesn't mean it's fault-free. All aspects of popular culture deserve thoughtful examination. Judge wisely.

Let us choose what is right. (Job 34:4)

Holy Lord, help me develop my faculties for critical thinking so that I may stay true to You and to myself.

Louis Armstrong's Barber

Joe Gibson recalls the visits that Louis Armstrong made to his barbershop in Corona, Queens, New York.

"He didn't like me to put him ahead of anybody," he says. "He would ask me how many customers I had, but he was never in a hurry."

Sometimes a kid would find Armstrong in the barbershop and run off to bring back friends. The legendary jazz man would joke with the kids, gently lecture them about staying in school, and take down each child's name and address. "He would later send each one a card," Gibson recalls.

Armstrong died on July 6, 1971, at his home in that same Queens neighborhood. Among the late musician's possessions was a manuscript entitled, "Barbershops," in which he touts Joe's place as his first choice for a haircut–and for good company.

Certain places feel welcoming. Treasure them.

The Lord is my shepherd...He makes me lie down in green pastures; He leads me beside still waters...He leads me in right paths. (Psalm 23:1,2,3)

Shepherd of the flock, bring us to Your pastures of peace and love.

Improving Women's Health

When Doctors Leo Lagasse and Robert Greenburg visited Africa in the 1990's, they were so moved by the suffering of women without medical care they started Medicine for Humanity.

"The health of women is so important," says Dr. Lagasse. "We directly improve the health of the whole community when we improve the health of women. When women are healthy, they gain confidence and they start leading. What we do...becomes an agent for improving society."

The non-profit gathers medical supplies and brings teams of volunteer physicians and nurses to 16 countries including South Africa, the Philippines and Costa Rica where they work with local doctors to provide needed medical care.

"We don't have failures, only different degrees of success. The only failure is if we don't go," says Dr. Lagasse.

Never stop caring about others.

Do not forget the birth pangs of your mother. Remember that it was of your parents you were born; how can you repay what they have given to you? (Sirach 7:27-28)

Encourage us to show our love for others through deeds on their behalf, Lord of Life.

Give Yourself a Break

You may not have time or money for a long vacation but you can "get away without going away" as Kristin Harmel, writing in *Women's Day*, puts it.

Hire someone else–to do today's chores

Bring the vacation to you–rent a travel video or DVD about a favorite locale; prepare the native cuisine and imagine yourself there.

Discover your hometown–play tourist. Learn about your neighborhood and surrounding area.

Get a massage–training schools offer inexpensive ones.

Escape with a book–bring an engrossing volume to lunch.

Take a class–what's new can challenge and refresh you.

Find a way to take a break regularly. It's good for the body and the spirit.

Jesus...said to them, "Come away to a deserted place all by yourselves and rest a while." (Mark 6:30,31)

Merciful Savior, encourage us to live less frenetically.

Helping in Another's Loss

When Kevin Bardsley learned that a Boy Scout was missing in Utah's mountains, he joined the search. "There had to be a different outcome this time," mused Bardsley. His own 12-year-old son Garrett had disappeared–and not been found–in those very same mountains.

"This is where I'm meant to be," Bardsley told Toby Hawkins, the dad of the missing boy, Brennan. He urged Hawkins to organize a press conference, calling for volunteers–something Bardsley, looking back, wished he had done.

The morning after Brennan went missing, 3,000 volunteers responded to the televised plea. By the next evening, Brennan was found.

"I know my son saved Brennan's life," Bardsley said. "Without the knowledge we gained searching for my son, we probably wouldn't have found him."

Helping others may help you heal. Who needs help today?

Kindred and helpers are for a time of trouble, but almsgiving rescues better than either. (Sirach 40:24)

I search for You, Master. Show me Your face. Grant me Your kindness.

Say No to Drugs with a Pharmacist's Help

Pharmacist Armon Neel has not worked behind a prescription counter for years. Instead, he specializes in working with patients to determine whether they are taking the right medication and/or the right dose. Sometimes, that involves helping patients avoid or reduce drug therapy.

Neel's profession affects his patients, particularly the elderly in nursing homes. "If I can get the drug therapy management for these patients correct," he says, "there are fewer hospital stays and admissions, lower costs and a better quality of life for the residents."

Neel's mission is to advance the idea that pharmacists must serve and protect the people who take the medications they dispense. "I get paid by the patient, not by the doctor," he says.

You life's work can also improve the lives of those you serve. How?

There are varieties of gifts, but the same Spirit...to each is given the manifestation of the Spirit for the common good.
(1 Corinthians 12:4,7)

Loving Lord, help me serve others through my work.

Growing Their Dreams

Maria Rodriguez proudly points to the flowerbeds she and her husband Hector tend in their Sunrise Garden.

Their mini-Eden, inside a white picket fence in the Patterson Houses public housing project in the Bronx, is the latest garden they have nurtured over the years. "We always had gardens, wherever we lived," Maria Rodriguez says.

This particular one is a masterpiece of recycling: planks, once used to ship plate glass, frame the flowerbeds; runners from an apartment now line one path; old fan blades have become large pinwheels. "It's beautiful," Hector Rodriguez says, admiring their achievement. Their garden thrives in a most unlikely place.

In our lives, with care and nurturing, our relationships—no matter how challenging at times—can also take root, flower and bring much joy.

Faithful friends are a sturdy shelter: whoever finds one has found a treasure. (Sirach 6:14)

You have made us stewards of Your creation, Creator. Remind us to cultivate the friends You give us as carefully as we cultivate Your earth.

Cheerful Givers

Robin and Kevin Maynard of Minneapolis. wondered how needy families could afford to buy their children birthday gifts.

Visiting a soup kitchen, Robin Maynard noticed a shelf of cake mixes so needy parents could prepare birthday cakes for their children.

Within a year the Maynards had spent $5,000 of their savings and formed Cheerful Givers, a nonprofit, to recruit volunteers and seek corporate donations. The volunteers buy, bag and deliver birthday gifts. To date they've distributed over 100,000 bags of stuffed animals, dolls and candy. All are anonymous so children will think their parents bought the gifts.

Says Robin Maynard, "In a perfect world, all families would be able to afford gifts for their kids."

This is not a perfect world. Help poor parents provide for their children.

If you then...know how to give good gifts to your children, how much more will your Father in heaven give good things to those who ask Him! (Matthew 7:11)

Forgive us for not doing more, God. Show us how to end poverty.

Get Some Sleep

Lack of sleep can prevent you from doing your best and can even be dangerous.

If you have trouble falling asleep, you're not alone. *Prevention* magazine cites National Institutes of Health estimates that one in three Americans has insomnia. Dr. Atul Malhotra of the Harvard Sleep Disorders Research Center offers these tips:

1. Eliminate caffeine for two weeks, including minor sources such as decaf coffee and chocolate. If this helps, make the change permanent. Some people are acutely caffeine sensitive.

2. Don't eat spicy or gassy foods; or too fast, to avoid indigestion.

3. Eat a light supper. Make lunch your largest meal.

4. Skip the pre-bed nightcap. Wine with dinner is OK, but alcohol just before bed can disrupt REM sleep.

5. Have a small bedtime snack to quiet a growling stomach.

Find what works best for you and get a good night's sleep.

Healthy sleep depends on moderate eating. (Sirach 31:20)

Bless us with sound, refreshing sleep, Creator.

Chilling Out

Many people have no memory of refrigerators without icemakers or automatic defrost systems. But our great-grandparents used iceboxes which used ice to cool food.

The iceman, often an immigrant, delivered ice from his horse-drawn cart. Hoisting a block of up to 100 pounds on his burlap or leather-protected shoulder was all in a day's work. And the ice from commercial ice companies was itself an improvement over the pond ice that too often became contaminated.

Expensive, cumbersome refrigerators were invented in the early 20th century, but it wasn't until the marketing of Frigidaire's chlorofluoro-carbon-cooled model in 1930 that people's food storage and eating habits changed. By the mid-1950's, over 80 percent of American households had their own 'fridge. Improvements in refrigerators have continued.

Indeed, change is a fact of life. Decide which changes and choices are right for you.

Choose with care. (1 Corinthians 3:10)

May innovations and technology be used for the common good, Spirit of Knowledge.

Do You Think Too Much?

Psychologist and author Susan Nolen-Hoeksema thinks some women obsess too much about appearance, relationships, health, etc. Here are her suggestions to keep worries in check:

- Be yourself; don't compare yourself to others.
- Don't let yourself believe the worst, but seek a brighter worldview.
- Have fun, relax, listen to music, go for a walk, pray, meditate.
- Aim only for realistic self-improvement, not impossible perfection.
- Be brave. Do not fear failure.
- Expand your circle of friends to include those who are positive and upbeat.
- Forgive. Give up anger, hatred and the desire for revenge.
- Let go of guilt. Do not let others make you feel guilty either.
- Talk to a wise and trusted friend when and if necessary.

Your life is worth enjoying and living.

Which of you...covets many days to enjoy good? Keep your tongue from evil...Do good; seek peace. (Psalm 34:12-13,14)

Increase women's self-esteem, Lord of Life.

Standing Firm for Equality

She was a 24 year old black woman, a teacher on her way to play the organ at the First Colored Congregational Church. She tried to board a New York City streetcar, despite laws forbidding African Americans from using public transportation. She was beaten by the conductor and street car driver and, with the assistance of a police officer, thrown to the street.

The woman was Elizabeth Jennings; the year 1854; and New York City streetcar conductors and drivers used whips to keep blacks from riding streetcars. Legal redress was usually unsuccessful.

But the well off and well connected Jennings pursued her case. Her attorney was future president Chester A. Arthur. Judge William Rockwell of the Brooklyn Circuit Court ruled that "Colored persons...had the same rights as others." A jury awarded Jennings about $250 damages.

Bigotry is always reprehensible. Every woman, man and youngster is God's well-loved child.

I took them up in My arms...I led them with cords of human kindness, with bands of love...I bent down to them and fed them. (Hosea 11:3,4)

Loving and sustaining Father, help us recognize that we are all members of the same family.

When Something Doesn't Seem Right

Tracie Dean couldn't shake the feeling that something was troubling the young girl she had met in an Alabama convenience store. Dean noticed a vacant stare in the child's eyes and spoke kindly to her. As she went to exit, the child tried to leave with her–until an older man stepped in.

Feeling uneasy, Dean wrote down the man's license plate and called 911 and checked missing-children websites. Eventually, she returned to the store to check their surveillance tapes. While she was there, a police officer came in and he promised to follow-up. They soon learned that the man Dean had seen with the child was a wanted sex offender.

Eventually, the man and a woman were arrested, and the girl put in foster care.

When questioned about her efforts, Tracie Dean said, "I just followed my heart." Our instincts can save us–or someone else–from trouble. Listen to your heart.

Walk with integrity of heart. (Psalm 101:2)

Show us how to protect the children the Father has entrusted to us from harm, Good Shepherd.

An Appeal Time Cannot Dilute

For most American art-lovers, Georgia O'Keefe embodies a unique balance of modernism and traditionalism in her style of painting. O'Keefe's paintings of large, blossoming flowers and breathtaking desert landscapes seems to symbolize and combine the new and the old.

Unlike some celebrated painters, O'Keefe enjoyed success very early on in her career. By 1927 and barely 40 years old, O'Keefe was supporting herself entirely by painting–very unusual for most artists, especially women.

Her broad appeal and the simplicity of her style lives on today, as attendance at exhibits highlighting her work have surged in recent years.

Freshness and talent are timeless. Don't let your unique abilities fall away. Nurture your gifts whenever and however possible.

To each is given the manifestation of the Spirit for the common good. (1 Corinthians 12:7)

Thank You for the abilities you have given me, Lord. Help me view them as a conduit to serving others.

Defining Genius

Although destined to create what has been called the most important British cultural achievement of his time, Samuel Johnson was a sickly child living in a "pinched and narrow world."

But Henry Hitchings writes admiringly of the famous lexicographer in *Defining the World: The Extraordinary Story of Dr. Johnson's Dictionary.* In over 42,000 entries, Johnson "mapped the contours of the (English) language... combining huge erudition with a steely wit."

Born in 1709, Johnson was blind in one eye, partially deaf, had facial scarring, and was periodically depressed.

Yet Johnson, who grew up in his family's bookshop and took refuge in words, overcame personal difficulties to write the first standard English dictionary, an innovative and critically acclaimed work.

What one person can achieve despite difficulties is amazing. Never stop doing what is good and right.

O Lord, we beseech You, give us success! (Psalm 118:25)

Remind us, Savior, that success is not lacking difficulties, but the overcoming of problems by Your grace.

Fulfilling the Dream of Music

Ever since she heard a recording of Yo-Yo Ma at the age of four, Clare Bradford wanted to be a cellist.

By the time she was seven, Bradford was playing in a Pittsburgh Symphony Orchestra master class.

She outgrew her quarter-size cello. Clare's parents were heartbroken when they learned that a new cello would cost more than $5,000. That was when Peter Jarvis, a local salesman, told them about a wealthy arts patron who sometimes bought instruments anonymously for college students.

The Bradfords videotaped Clare's performances and Jarvis passed the tape on to a possible donor. Clare has since received two cellos from the generous benefactor making it possible for her to follow her dream.

Your dreams will find a way of coming true if you believe in them enough. And don't forget to return the favor.

Hope does not disappoint us. (Romans 5:5)

Inspire musically gifted children to practice diligently and hope fervently, Holy Wisdom.

Building a Platform for Life

During her first term as Atlanta's mayor, Shirley Franklin raised sales tax by one percentage point, eliminated more than 1,000 city jobs, and spent her time talking potholes and sewers.

"If you look in a book on how to get re-elected, it's kind of like the not-to-do list," says the first African-American woman to serve as mayor of a major southern U.S. city.

And yet her approval ratings exceed 75 percent.

"I'm kind of an unintentional politician," Franklin explains, adding that she finds herself more concerned with policy than with political strategy.

Franklin chose to run for office when she realized that she herself wasn't following the career advice she was giving to young women. "I felt I had an obligation to break through the barrier," she says.

No matter what our work, we need to challenge ourselves and those around us to choose the common good.

Give the members of your community a fair hearing. (Deuteronomy 1:16)

You are my hope, my God, I place all my trust in You.

John Leguizamo and the Fresh Air Fund

Many know John Leguizamo as an actor, comedian, writer and producer. But before he was an accomplished professional, he was a poor eight-year-old kid sent by his family for a vacation in Rhode Island courtesy of the Fresh Air Fund which helps urban youngsters escape the city's heat and experience rural life.

"All I could think of was: 'My parents are getting rid of me'," Leguizamo says. "They are finally fulfilling their promise that they were going to send me away if I misbehave, and I'm never going to come back."

Actually his family wanted him to have a good summer experience and he did. As a *New York Times* story notes, "He made friends, harvested the local strawberry patch, swam and fished in a nearby stream and a lake."

How can you help poor youngsters enjoy this summer?

The streets of the city shall be full of boys and girls playing. (Zechariah 8:5)

Bless teachers, camp counselors, pediatricians, and all who work with children, Abba.

Taking Care While Giving Care

Debbie Sensabaugh quit her job as a special education teacher to care full-time for her terminally-ill son Gregory. "But I can be the world's worst when it comes to taking care of myself," she says.

Gary Klock echoes that sentiment, touting himself as the poster child for how not to treat yourself while you're caring for an ailing family member.

While giving care, it is critical to schedule time to take care of yourself, explains Carmel Murphy-Norris, caregiver manager for Valley Program for Aging Services in Virginia. "Caregiving is good only if the caregiver is healthy," she says.

A support network of family and friends helps—as does making it a practice to reach out to them. Talking through your feelings, fears and frustrations is also good—especially with God.

We are called to love our neighbor, but Jesus told us to do so "as we love ourselves."

Jesus went throughout Galilee...curing every disease and every sickness....They brought to Him all...who were afflicted with various diseases and pains. (Matthew 4:23,24)

Lord, help me when my day is long, my patience is short and when loving is difficult.

Being Kind to Dopey

A mother and daughter, making their way through Disney World on a hot summer afternoon, met Dopey the dwarf character. Seeing a line next to him, but not approaching the costumed-figure, the mother inquired as to where the line began.

"You can go ahead," responded a mother at the front of the long line. "Yes," said a parent behind her, "We're waiting for Snow White. We don't want to see Dopey."

Hearing that, the little girl ran to Dopey and hugged him, saying: "We love you too, Dopey! We love you a lot!"

Suddenly, the two heard a voice behind them say: "And I love you, Dopey!" It was Snow White herself, who then told mother and daughter, "Let's all take a picture together!"

Every single person we meet is special. Embrace the opportunity to experience the glimpse of God's goodness found in every heart.

Love your neighbor as yourself. (Mark 12:31)

Help me recognize Your goodness, Master, in everyone I meet today.

To Save a Life

Police Officer Erik Hansen knew his partner's life depended on his actions. It was a July afternoon in New York's East Harlem neighborhood, and he found himself the target of a gunman who had already wounded his partner, Lt. Patrick O'Boyle.

With only a fire hydrant to shield him, Officer Hansen engaged in a gunfight with the suspect. Then, though shot in the ankle, he pursued the gunman into a building until the gunman jumped from a 14th floor window.

For his courageous efforts, Hansen received an outpouring of compassion from the community and was nominated for the New York's Finest Medal. Amazed by community support, the heroic police office said his "primary concern was protecting Pat."

We all experience times when we are wounded and vulnerable. Let's each pray for the courage to help one another in such trying situations.

Each one helps the other, saying to one another, "Take courage!" (Isaiah 41:6)

Who needs my help, Holy Spirit? Who needs my courage?

Lemons, Lemonade and a Legacy

She was diagnosed with aggressive pediatric cancer as an infant. When she was four-years-old Alexandra Scott started a lemonade stand to raise money for cancer research.

With the help of family and friends, her idea caught on. At her death four years later, Alex, as her family called her, had raised more than $900,000.

Alex's parents, Liz and Jay Scott, formed the Alex's Lemonade Stand Foundation. More than 4,000 lemonade stands have been established around the world. And they've raised $5 million dollars for cancer research. Her father says that they have one goal—"To grow until we're out of business."

No matter how short a person's earthly life, their spirit and their goodness can live on.

In the memory of virtue is immortality, because it is known both by God and by mortals. (Wisdom of Solomon 4:1)

Gentle Jesus, inspire researchers to find cures for cancers.

More than a War Story

Richard Dobbins has taken on a labor of love which he expects to last a lifetime.

Along with a few employees, the former mutual-fund manager is creating the Civil War Research Database documenting the lives of the war's four million enlisted men.

Since 1993, Dobbins has keyed-in induction dates, promotions, combat service, causes of death and other personnel records from nearly 200 sources. Once all the basic demographic data is entered, Dobbins plans to add more details and to invite contributions from historians and families.

Ultimately, the database will be capable of fleshing out the stories of all those who fought in the Civil War, not just the presidents, generals and chiefs.

The lives of ordinary people who "gave the last full measure of devotion" are supremely important. Their stories must be told and remembered.

Let us now sing the praises of...our ancestors. (Sirach 44:1)

May our nation, under You, Eternal God, "have a new birth of freedom."

Hold on to Courage

Here's an old tale that's worth retelling: The devil was displaying various tools his followers should use to mislead human beings. The impressive array included Pride, Hatred, Jealousy, Dishonesty and Impurity.

Next to these was a smaller, less noticeable tool. One of the minor devils asked, "What's the name of this one, and of what use can it be?" "Oh, a most valuable instrument, I assure you," Satan answered. "It always works when the others fail. It's called Discouragement."

It's hard to go through life without getting discouraged occasionally. Yet allowing ourselves to be downhearted not only keeps us from getting our task done–whatever it may be–it prevents us from experiencing the joy God wants us to know.

If things are really rough, seek help. And trust God who will always be there for us.

Trust in the steadfast love of God. (Psalm 52:8)

Give me a heart of hope, Blessed Trinity. Encompass me with Your compassion.

Jazz Treasure Trove

As a boy, Frank Driggs listened to jazz on the radio. After college, he moved to New York City and listened to live music at the Savoy Ballroom and Birdland.

Over the years, this son of a jazz musician lovingly built a collection of jazz-related posters, recordings, ticket stubs and photos of musical greats Louis Armstrong, Duke Ellington, Billie Holiday, Count Basie and Benny Goodman among others.

This memorabilia, which one expert characterizes as having tremendous depth, is "a unique assemblage of jazz materials you won't find anywhere else," according to Dan Morgenstern, director of the Institute of Jazz Studies.

"Frank had the foresight and advantage to acquire these materials from the musicians and their estates, and now that they're all gone, he has this unique, one-of-a-kind treasure trove."

Whether with fond memories, photos, or other cherished items, each of us can put together our own unique treasure trove of loving memories.

The memory of the righteous is a blessing. (Proverbs 10:7)

May we treasure our families' histories in photos, mementos and fondly told stories, Abba.

The Bonus of Beauty Within

As shallow as it may sound, many people believe that their lives would be perfect if they were more beautiful.

Psychoanalyst Sigmund Freud, in discussing those who seek happiness in life through the enjoyment of beauty, says "beauty has no obvious use; nor is there any cultural necessity for it. Yet civilization could not do without it." Why?

There is a world of difference between looking beautiful outside and being beautiful within. Katherine Ann Porter says "the real sin against life is to abuse and destroy beauty, even one's own... for that has been put in our care and we are responsible for its well-being." We don't have to be perfect for God to love us; for God loves us just as we are. And Anne Frank once said, "Think of all the beauty left around you and still be happy."

It's good advice. Appreciate the beauty already inside you.

The glory of the stars is the beauty of heaven...Look at the rainbow...it is exceedingly beautiful....He scatters the snow like birds flying down...the eye is dazed by the beauty of its whiteness. (Sirach 43:9,11,17)

Lord, help me to learn that it's from You all life's blessings and beauty flow.

The Importance of Not Showing Up

Our fast-paced, results-driven society has made "vacation" a bad word.

In fact, in some companies, workers are rewarded for forfeiting earned vacation days. Workers in 2004 alone gave up 415 million vacation days they "couldn't find time to use."

That's a worrying trend according to experts, who say that forfeiting vacation time can make you more stressed and less efficient at work.

Instead of skipping your vacation time...

- Take a vacation day when away on business. Take one full day pursuing a pleasurable activity, like golfing or sight-seeing.
- Ask for a "half-day" vacation on Fridays or Mondays, to extend the weekend.
- Take one-day mid-week vacations to do something special—or curl up on your couch.

It's important to break up your demanding work week.

Six days shall work be done; but the seventh is a sabbath of complete rest. (Leviticus 23:3)

I pray I don't let work's demands interfere with the rest of my life, Spirit of God.

Fighting to the Right Finish

Fannie Lou Hamer, the granddaughter of a slave, just wanted to vote. But in August, 1962, when she and 17 other African Americans tried to register to vote at the Indianola, Mississippi, courthouse they was arrested and jailed.

Almost a year later, she and other civil rights workers were arrested, jailed and beaten in Winona, Mississippi. But Fannie Lou Hamer was not deterred. At the 1964 Democratic national convention in Atlantic City, New Jersey, she challenged the Mississippi delegation for not representing all Mississippians. Her testimony was broadcast nationwide, alerting the nation to the struggle for voting rights in the south.

A year later, President Lyndon Johnson signed the Voting Rights Act of 1965.

Remember, the denial of even one person's right to vote or to civil rights imperils your own. Stand up for what is right.

You...repented and did what was right in My sight by proclaiming liberty to one another... but then you...profaned My Name when each of you took back your...slaves. (Jeremiah 34:15,16)

Just Judge, be our strength as we choose to treat each other as brothers and sisters, as equals.

Stand Up and Sing

"Take me out to the ballgame…"

The seventh-inning stretch would not be the same without singing that tune. But, few know that the song refers to a baseball-crazy young woman who wants to go to a game with her boyfriend. The song was written in 1908 by Jack Norworth, a song and dance man appearing in the Ziegfeld Follies who thought it would make a good number for the show. His friend Albert Von Tilzer supplied the music. Neither man had ever seen a baseball game.

Within two years, it was being sung in ballparks across the country. By the time Norworth and Von Tilzer died in the 1950's, "Take Me Out to the Ballgame" was America's third most performed song, following "The Star-Spangled Banner" and "Happy Birthday."

The simplest choices you make or actions you take might be more important than you know. Do your best in everything.

The Lord…will dwell in the midst of Jerusalem…And the streets of the city shall be full of boys and girls playing in its streets. (Zechariah 8:3,5)

Jesus, as a boy You must have enjoyed games and music and the everyday pleasures of life. Help us to do the same.

Meet a Healer At Work

"She is completely present when she's speaking with you," says a colleague of Dr. Adele O'Sullivan. "You come away feeling good about yourself, that you're cared for."

Dr. O'Sullivan is also a Sister of St. Joseph of Carondelet and was named the 2006 Family Physician of the year by the American Academy of Family Physicians. Among the reasons for the award is her strong commitment to treating the homeless.

She is medical director for Maricopa County's Health Care for the Homeless program in Arizona. The county is the nation's fourth most populous and has about 13,000 homeless residents. Dr. O'Sullivan also treats about 3,000 every year at Phoenix's Andre House soup kitchen. She also brings her medical training and a portable drugstore to soup kitchens, resource centers and the streets so the neediest receive the care they need and deserve.

People need healing of body and soul. Be willing to be an instrument of God's grace for the good of His children.

Physicians...pray to the Lord that He grant them success in diagnosis and in healing, for the sake of preserving life. (Sirach 38:13,14)

Grace us with many wise and caring doctors, Lord of Life.

Write Grandma a What?

Write Grandma a What? was the headline of a newspaper story about the decline in the fine art of letter writing. Young people in particular seem to communicate primarily by cell phone, text messaging and email.

"Why would anyone write a letter?" a Harvard graduate student was quoted as saying. "It simply takes too long. You have to write it, print it, find an envelope and stamp, get to the mail drop and then wait for a response."

So why write? Because letters are personal. And because they're so rare, receiving a letter is special.

"Traditional letter writing made us take the time to think of what we wanted to say, and how to say it, and what impact it would have on the person receiving it," says Naomi Baron, a linguistics professor at the American University.

Give joy and surprise to someone you know. Write a letter.

He brought the letter to the king of Israel, which read, 'When this letter reaches you, know that I have sent to you my servant Naaman". (2 Kings 5:6)

Remind us, God, that a letter is always a unique, personal and welcome gift.

Let's Be Honest

"Creeping crookedness" is what Rev. Eugene Laubach called the attitude that everybody should just look out for themselves. How should a person of faith view honesty?

While serving at New York's Riverside Church, the minister said that a person of faith believes that he or she "lives in a moral universe where a lie will not endure forever and where trust and integrity are the real name of the game."

A person of faith, Rev. Laubach adds, "believes that the goal of life in not just to get, but to give, that people are responsible for one another under the one God who is Father of all, that there are some objective truths that cannot be brushed aside. ...Perhaps the first question we need ask about mass dishonesty is whose world we really think we're living in."

We know the answer: this is God's world and He invites us to live our lives honestly and honorably.

If you choose, you can keep the commandments, and to act faithfully is a matter of your own choice. (Sirach 15:15)

Spirit of Truth, fill me with Your wisdom and grace so that I will choose what is right.

Making Connections

The number of adopted Chinese children in the United States has grown to over 45,000 with thousands more added annually, according to *People* magazine.

And thanks to adoptions networks, Web sites, and DNA registries, American parents are searching for, and more confident about finding, their youngsters' biological siblings.

Current genetic tests can identify only identical twins with 100% certainty. Otherwise, science is somewhat less reliable in determining whether any two youngsters are actually siblings.

Nevertheless, there is often a palpable connection when some children are introduced. "We're sisters! Yes! We're sisters!" shrieked Renee to her fraternal twin, Annie. Their families stay in touch and marvel at their girls' similarities.

As amazing as it may be to meet a brother or sister for the first time, it's really our love and connectedness that is most important. We are all God's children.

You, O Lord, are our Father; our Redeemer from of old is Your Name. (Isaiah 63:16)

Father, we are Your children; brothers and sisters to one another. Remind us to treat one another with deepest respect.

Do It Anyway

Here are some thoughts about the challenges of leadership:

1. People can be illogical, unreasonable and self-centered. Love them.

2. Do good and you'll be accused of ulterior motives. Do good.

3. Be successful and you'll win false friends and true enemies. Succeed.

4. The good you do today will be forgotten tomorrow. Do it.

5. Honesty makes you vulnerable. Be honest.

6. The biggest people with the biggest ideas can be shot down by the littlest people with the littlest ideas. Think big.

7. People favor underdogs, but follow only top dogs. Fight for a few underdogs.

8. What takes years building may be destroyed overnight. Build.

9. People really need help, but may attack if you help them. Help them.

10. Give the world your best—no matter what.

You are safe. Be strong and courageous. (Daniel 10:19)

Redeemer, enable me to be a leader in every aspect of my life. But always to follow You.

The House that Verdi Built

In 1889, Italian composer Giuseppe Verdi purchased land in Milan. On it he built a large Venetian-style palazzo with spacious rooms, artists' studios, a concert hall, a library and a grand dining room.

Verdi's dream was to establish a retirement home for musicians and other performers as well as teachers and directors. Although he and his wife died before seeing *Casa di Riposo* open, today it's just what the composer envisioned: a home for singers, dancers, musicians, conductors, teachers, directors and anyone else who has established their careers on the stage.

Residents pay rent on a sliding scale according to what they can afford. In recent years, music students have taken up short-term residence at the Casa—learning from the masters who are their neighbors.

What we build, tangible or intangible, remains as our lasting memorial.

Rise before the aged. (Leviticus 19:32)

Generous Creator, may all our works give You praise.

A Nickel, Coffee, and Inspiration

New York City ranks as one of the haute-cuisine capitols of the world. But from 1912 to the early 1960s, it was also home to Horn and Hardart's Automats, restaurants where a nickel would buy the most down-and-out patrons a cup of coffee.

The food was good and inexpensive, and the novelty of being able to put a coin in a slot and pull out a ready-made sandwich or hot meal drew a steady stream of customers, both of modest means and wealthy, for decades.

In the middle of the Great Depression, famed songwriter Irving Berlin was in a creative slump when he sat in an Automat watching the patrons. They exhibited American optimism in better times to come. Inspired, the result was Berlin's "Let's Have Another Cup of Coffee," one of the biggest hits of his career.

Cultivate your sense of optimism—and be refreshed.

Abound in hope. (Romans 15:13)

Thank You, God, for Your gift of hope.

If You Would Rather Be Unhappy...

We want to be happy, but sometimes we sabotage ourselves by focusing on the negative. Here are ten ways to be miserable:

1. Concentrate on the bad things in life, not the good.
2. Put an excessive value on money.
3. Believe you're indispensable to your job, community or friends.
4. Feel you're overburdened and that people take advantage of you.
5. Decide you're exceptional and entitled to special privileges.
6. Think you can control your nerves by will power.
7. Forget the feelings and rights of other people.
8. Cultivate a pessimistic outlook.
9. Never overlook a slight or forget a grudge.
10. And don't forget to feel sorry for yourself.

If you'd rather be happy, remember that you can be realistic about life and still be positive.

There is nothing on earth that I desire other than You...God is the strength of my heart and my portion forever. (Psalm 73:25,26)

Remind me that You are the source of all joy, Spirit of Love.

Thinking Outside the Box

At first, Australian-born builder Rob Leslie rejected a request to design a house that's hurricane-proof, withstands earthquakes up to 6.9 on the Richter scale, sleeps eight people, takes less than a day to construct—and costs $1,000.

But two weeks after he was challenged, Leslie woke up with an idea. With a compass, he drew a circle on a piece of drafting paper—and his design was born. Then he and his son went outside the family's Minnesota home and, in a few hours, built a prototype of the "roundhouse."

More than 600 roundhouses have been built worldwide. And since 80 percent of the world's traditional housing is round, these permanent structures are ones people are happy to live in.

Sometimes we're faced with a seemingly impossible task. It's never too late to go back to the drawing board—and emerge with the answer after all!

> **The necessities of life are water, bread, and clothing, and also a house to assure privacy. (Sirach 29:21)**

> *Be present in my home, Creator. May Your love fill its rooms; fill my heart!*

Finding the Sacred Within

Carl McColman, author of *Spirituality: Where Body and Soul Encounter the Sacred* suggests that "to foster...wonder and openness and an awareness of the Sacred" we ought to:

- Pray or meditate daily
- Engage in spiritual reading and study
- Join a healthy faith community
- Engage in a personal improvement program
- Honor some form of Sabbath
- Maintain a sense of humor
- Relate charitably to the needy
- Interact with persons from other traditions

As McColman writes, spirituality involves a choice: "to live life out of wonder rather than self-protection...to be open to belief in God...to nurture a relationship with God...to engage in community building, peacemaking and sacrifice."

Our steps are made firm by the Lord...the Lord holds us by the hand. (Psalm 37:23,24)

Guide my relationship with You, Holy Trinity, one God.

Rising above Adversity

Liz Murray grew up with cocaine-addicted parents. There were always drugs, but never any food. By age 15, her mother had died of AIDS, her father was on the streets and so was she. But she was accepted at Humanities Preparatory Academy, a public high school, took a double course load and studied in a stairwell.

Despite being homeless, forced to sleep and study in the subway, Murray did extraordinarily well in high school. She applied for a $12,000-a-year *New York Times* college scholarship and at 19 became a Harvard University undergrad.

As Liz Murray said on visiting Harvard University with her high school, "Why can't this be mine if I really want it?"

That attitude is what we each need if we are to become all we can be; if we are to become more fully our truest selves.

The Lord...has saved my life from every adversity. (1 Kings 1:29)

Abba, parenting well is the most important job on earth. Support all parents, especially those who are struggling.

Life's Twists and Turns

Vonetta Flowers of Birmingham, Alabama grew up knowing she had athletic ability and sure she was destined for the Summer Olympics in track and field.

What she learned was that life can take some unusual twists and turns. "You can be a great runner," her coach told her at age nine. "But it takes more than just running fast. It takes believing in yourself and your potential."

In time, Vonetta found her specialty was the long jump. As an All-American on an athletic scholarship she was a likely prospect for the Olympics until life and sports injuries interfered. She was devastated. "Everything I'd worked for was gone."

But it wasn't all gone. Flowers retrained and realized her potential. As a member of the women's bobsled team she won the gold at the Winter Olympics.

Stay open to life's changes. What may seem devastating one day could turn into a wonderful opportunity the next.

Happy are those who persevere. (Daniel 12:12)

Life and illnesses and injuries can overwhelm us, Jesus. Give us the grace to persevere in becoming all we can be.

Let Us Pray

They have different names in different churches–prayer chains, prayer trees, prayer ministry, ministry of praise–but the work is the same. Volunteers pray for anyone who asks.

Many church ministries need people to help in a very active way, but, by its nature, even those confined to home can pray.

"I started in this when I was in my late 20s and had three little kids," says Lora Shoen, the prayer tree coordinator for St. Raphael parish in Rockville, Maryland. "This is a wonderful way for people to participate who can't come in and volunteer. They're doing something important."

Absolutely anyone can ask for and receive prayers. Confidentiality is key. Shoen, a cancer survivor who welcomed prayers, adds, "We have a parish of believers. That's how we help each other."

Pray for your neighbors, for all who need God's strength and blessings.

Father, hallowed be your Name. Your kingdom come. Give us each day our daily bread. And forgive us our sins, for we ourselves forgive everyone indebted to us. And do not bring us to the time of trial. (Luke 11:2-4)

Spirit of Faith, help me pray for the good of all Your people.

Playtime Isn't Over—It's Just Beginning!

Nowadays, it seems most people are stretched t-h-i-n when it comes to work demands, family obligations and stress. In a wired-for-productivity, "24/7" world, where work never ceases, who has time for fun?

Not Americans! According to a recent survey, America's leisure time has decreased a whopping 37 percent since 1973. Over the same period, the average workweek has jumped from under 41 hours to nearly 47 hours.

Experts agree that a life where play, leisure and fun balance work and other obligations can help you live an overall busy life while warding off serious, stress-related repercussions.

Playtime *is* beneficial to your overall health. Make daily opportunities to enjoy leisure time. Restore balance to your life.

I commend enjoyment for there is nothing better for people...than to eat, and drink, and enjoy themselves, for this will go with them in their toil. (Ecclesiastes 8:15)

I pray for relief from daily stresses, Lord. Help me make and take time for play, for rest, for relaxation.

Marie Curie–Tragedy and Glory

As a teen, Barbara Goldsmith, who idolized Marie Curie, had a photo of her with her arms wrapped around her young daughters.

Goldsmith's admiration wasn't because of Madame's Curie's discoveries, but because her mother was "in the hospital, recovering from a car crash," Goldsmith writes in *Obsessive Genius: The Inner World of Marie Curie.* "I wanted my mother to hold me, but she couldn't." So Goldsmith looked up to Curie as "the strongest and most capable woman in the world."

Madame Curie was strong and capable. Her mother died when she was 10. She left her native Poland and graduated from the Sorbonne. She and her husband Pierre won the 1903 Nobel Prize in physics for discovering radium. Widowed, Madame Curie won another Nobel for isolating radium and polonium. These discoveries probably caused her death in 1934.

Be as strong and capable as you can–for your sake, for others.

Give her a share in the fruit of her hands, and let her works praise her in the city gates. (Proverbs 31:31)

Creator, bless all scientists and help them work for the peace and welfare of the world.

Resilience: Nature or Nurture?

It seems some people possess a terrific ability to rebound from life's difficulties, even the big ones. Others seem to struggle with even the most mundane of daily irritations. Are some people born with an innate ability to "bounce back?"

Nan Henderson, co-founder of Resiliency in Action, a publishing company, believes resilience is a skill which can be learned and nurtured. She offers these "resiliency building" tips:

- Adopt a "strength perspective," in which you exercise and focus on your strengths, not your weaknesses.

- Set high but realistic expectations for success. Identify and pursue steps toward progress, not perfection.

- Contribute to others. One of the best ways to rebound from personal setbacks is to help someone else with theirs.

Resiliency implies a conscious decision not to give up on life—your own or another's.

Be courageous and valiant. (2 Samuel 13:28)

Help me keep sight of the important role I play when I am strong for those who are not, Abba.

Why Forgive?

It's been said that harboring resentment is like taking poison–and expecting the other person to die.

When someone injures us and we hold on to the hurt, we cannot love that person. We build a wall between us, and to some extent, others as well. Forgiveness frees the forgiver–and the person who did something wrong, but now welcomes forgiveness–to love and grow.

In *A Wedding Sermon,* Rev. Dietrich Bonhoeffer wrote, "Live together in the forgiveness of your sins for without it no human fellowship...can survive. Don't insist on your rights, don't blame each other, don't judge or condemn each other, don't find fault with each other, but take one another as you are, and forgive each other every day from the bottom of your hearts."

Forgiveness can heal your spirit and your relationships. In time, forgiveness can even relieve the pain of memory.

Forgive, and you will be forgiven. (Luke 6:37)

Heal my heart and soul, Merciful Jesus. Help me to ask for forgiveness and to offer forgiveness for my sake, for the sake of the other person and for You who forgive us both.

Seeking Our Potential

More than 5,000 applicants answered the following want ad that appeared in a London newspaper in 1914: "Men wanted for hazardous journey—small wages, bitter cold, long months of complete darkness, constant danger, safe return doubtful. Honor and recognition in case of success."

For the 28 men chosen by Sir Ernest Shackleton for his Antarctic expedition, it was indeed a "hazardous journey." Their ship, the *Endurance* was crushed by ice and the crew endured short supplies and countless difficulties before they triumphed over the elements. All 28 survived and returned home two years after their quest began.

Every human being has a potential bit of greatness within, put there by God. But without adequate challenge, such potential may lie dormant and that person will never achieve all that's really possible.

Make every effort to fulfill the mission which God has entrusted to you and you alone.

To one he gave five talents, to another two, to another one, to each according to his ability. (Matthew 25:15)

Jesus, help me follow in Your footsteps whatever the cost.

He Takes the Cake

Raven Patrick De'Sean Dennis III, aka Cake Man Raven, thinks big.

After graduating from Providence Rhode Island's Johnson & Wales culinary school, Dennis began building his Cake Man reputation. He has been commissioned to bake cakes for the birthdays of Lena Horne, Ella Fitzgerald, Dizzy Gillespie, Cab Calloway, and more. For hip-hop artist Mary J. Blige's birthday, the cake was four feet wide and two feet tall. It included a CD, a shopping bag, a purse, cosmetics and a dove – all edible of course.

Dennis has also baked and decorated a 7-foot-tall, 12-foot-long edible Brooklyn Bridge for that famous edifice's 120th birthday.

Today, Dennis bakes, decorates, teaches, and trains his young staff in everything from the fine art of cake decorating to the importance of proper attire.

Every person, every generation needs the chance to dream big.

**Teach and admonish one another.
(Colossians 3:16)**

Enable teachers to help youngsters on their way to success, Abba.

Out of a Shared Experience, Compassion

Homelessness is part of both Dr. Anna Lou Dehavenon's past and her present.

A research scientist who has dedicated the last 25 years to homelessness and hunger in her native New York City, Dr. Dehavenon spends most of each day dealing with homeless families.

Years ago as a 26-year-old widow with two small children, she herself had been homeless and without an extended family. She leaned on friends for help. "I had been homeless," she realized. "It never occurred to me at the time, only when looking back."

Homelessness and hardships can strike anyone, anytime. Show compassion to the needy. One day, you might be walking in their shoes.

In everything do to others as you would have them do to you; for this is the Law and the Prophets. (Matthew 7:12)

Merciful Savior, imbue us with Your own righteous indignation at the poverty in the midst of our abundance.

Still Helpful After All These Years

Jimmie Garner's helping hand has spanned decades.

The pattern of pitching in started for this 91-year-old from Ardmore, Oklahoma, early in his teaching career. Day-to-day conversations made him aware that some young people might be having problems that went beyond difficulties with math or reading. He offered to help with lunch money or just as a sympathetic listener.

"I never left a kid hungry," Garner recalled.

In the years since his retirement, he continues to help out "wherever and whenever I can." Recent projects have included repairing a broken seat on an antique rocking horse, donating time to projects that benefit area youth, and getting involved with fundraising for non-profit organizations

In life, it's never too late to lend a hand. At any age, you need only an open heart, ready to give.

O give thanks to the God of gods, for His steadfast love endures forever. (Psalm 136:2)

All the days of our lives, Lord, I give thanks for Your many moment-by-moment kindnesses.

Who Was Emmett Till?

Emmett Till was 14 years old in August, 1955 when he went to visit his Mississippi relatives.

According to news stories, the black youngster likely flirted with a white woman, breaking the local code of interracial conduct. The woman's husband and others kidnapped Till. Less than a week later his maimed body was recovered from the Tallahatchie River, a 70-pound fan hanging around his neck by barbed wire.

Till's mother, Mamie Till-Mobley defied the sheriff and had her son's body returned to Chicago and waked in an open coffin. The widely reported event led to the largest civil rights demonstration up to that time in the U.S.

"Mrs. Mobley did a profound strategic thing," said Jesse Jackson after her death in 2003 at 81, by allowing the world to see "his body water-soaked and defaced."

The evils of prejudice and violence still exist. Every single person has the responsibility to build tolerance and peace. Do all you can.

He asked Jesus, "And who is my neighbor?" Jesus replied, "A man was going down from Jerusalem to Jericho...a Samaritan...was moved with pity." (Luke 10:29-30,33)

Enable me to eliminate my biases, Creator.

What's on Your List?

After author and television host Phil Keoghan had a near-death experience, he wrote down all the things he wanted to do. "I urge others to pursue their dreams," Keoghan says. "Start by writing them down."

Here are his tips for developing your "wish list for life."

- **Make it uniquely yours.** Create a list based on experiences that have had special meaning for you.
- **Go public.** Share your list with your spouse, friends and children.
- **Make time for dreams–and lose the guilt.** Having adventures is not a waste of time, but a way to maximize our limited time on earth.
- **Begin NOW.** Get started on living your wish list right away.

No one is guaranteed a tomorrow. We owe it to our Creator to make the most of the moments of our life every day.

I came that they may have life, and have it abundantly. (John 10:10)

Enable me, Lord of Life, to drink deeply from the wellsprings of life in You and with You.

A Garden Grows and So Does a Child

Nature has a way of nurturing our spirits. And Dr. Sebastiano Santostefano tapped into this in his work with traumatized children.

After a distinguished career at Harvard Medical School and prestigious psychiatric facilities, he and his wife, Susan, a counselor, founded the Institute for Child and Adolescent Development in an 1886 house surrounded by a sloping one-acre yard with centenarian trees.

They hired a landscape architect. In *Child Therapy in the Great Outdoors,* Santostefano describes how the babbling brook, pond, hills, woods and stretches of open field have became the "office" where troubled children have a chance to heal.

Anyone who has spent time amidst the glories of nature knows how refreshing and therapeutic that can be. So, lunch in a park. Enjoy a sunset or sunrise with a loved one. Delight in God's good earth.

You make springs gush forth in the valleys...giving drink to every wild animal...By the streams the birds...have their habitation. (Psalm 104:10,11,12)

Holy Spirit, remind us that our ancestral home was a garden, and that nature is where we'll find healing, beauty and refreshment.

Doing Good Is Good for You

Studies show that volunteers reap important rewards by helping others. For example, "it's one of the best ways people over 60 can contribute to their own well-being," says Linda Fried, director of the Center on Aging and Health at Johns Hopkins University, who has studied the benefits of volunteering.

Child psychologists also report that volunteer work helps young people increase self-esteem and learn valuable socialization skills.

"There's nothing like giving to someone else and realizing you are strengthening the fundamental fabric of society," says Diana Aviv, president of the Independent Sector. "Volunteering increases a person's sense of responsibility…"

A woman who found she was slipping into sedentary retirement cherishes her life's direction after she became a literacy volunteer. "The children and the friends I've made through this organization are like angels to me. I just want to keep on giving."

Consider becoming a volunteer today.

Faith by itself, if it has no works, is dead. (James 2:17)

Enlighten my search for volunteer opportunities, Father of all. Help me serve You by serving others.

Keys to a Healthier Life

By now most of us have a good idea of what we need to do to live a healthier life. Nevertheless, according to Janis Graham, writing in *Good Housekeeping*, the advice bears repeating.

1. Live an active life.
2. Pay attention to those extra pounds.
3. Say 'yes' to more fruits and vegetables.
4. Get doctor-recommended cancer screenings.
5. If you smoke, quit.

There are no new ideas here, just tried and true guidelines toward healthier living. The only thing missing may be the discipline and support needed whenever you wish to replace a bad habit with a better one. It's not easy to change habits, but it's always possible. Take good care of yourself.

Health and fitness are better than any gold, and a robust body than countless riches. (Sirach 30:15)

It's difficult to change unhealthy but established habits, Jesus. Give us Your strength to make needed changes.

When Helping Becomes a Challenge

When Hurricane Katrina came ashore over the Gulf Coast on August 29, 2005, Jay and Vicki Brooks got ready–for the fourth time in five years.

The Baton Rouge, Louisiana couple, their three children and two dogs were familiar with opening their home to relatives and other evacuees displaced by hurricanes, floods and other disasters, sometimes for an extended period of time.

But after Hurricane Katrina, they took eight relatives and three dogs into their four bedroom, three bathroom house.

"I'm sure we get on one another's nerves, but we're trying very hard to respect each other's space," said Vicki Brooks. Despite the strain, lack of privacy and inconvenience, the couple say that, "When all is said and done, we will be closer for this and grateful that we had the ability to do this for our family."

Helping others isn't always a walk in the park. But it can be incredibly rewarding.

Be doers of the word, and not merely hearers. (James 1:22)

Christ Jesus, it won't always be easy, but help me emulate You when I serve family and others in need.

Retired, at the Ripe Old Age of 14

Most people consider retiring when they reach their 60s or 70s. A few, in their 50s. But how about at age 14?

Devan Osterhout, a teenage entrepreneur, had already "retired" from one successful business career by the time he was 14 years old.

In order to help his family pay his tuition at a private school, Devan decided to start a bottle and can collection and return business. Devan's ingenuity and perseverance helped turn the business into something special.

Devan recruited the help of various businesses in his area, asking the owners to save cans and bottles for him. He did the same with a number of college groups and student organizations, as well as several apartment complexes. Eventually, Devan was earning enough to pay a full year's tuition. He donated the remaining money to a shelter. Devan "retired" when high school demanded too much of his time.

The next time you have a good idea, make it happen.

**The clever do all things intelligently.
(Proverbs 13:16)**

Help me believe in myself, in Your gifts to me, Holy Spirit.

Music for Hope

Like so many others, Elliott Glick watched helplessly as the waters of Hurricanes Katrina and Rita drowned the Gulf States, particularly New Orleans.

As the owner of the Starving Artist Café and Gallery, a City Island, New York, coffeehouse and art gallery, he showcased musicians–singer-songwriters, jazz and blues artists–who could trace their influences right back to that region.

"I started to think that maybe we could use that music…from New Orleans to give something back to them when they needed it," Glick said. He organized a six-hour outdoor concert "Music for Hope: A Concert for the Gulf States." When the last note was played, there was $1,000 in contributions for Habitat for Humanity.

Even in life's darkest days there is always a note of hope; a desire to make a difference.

The God of Jacob is our refuge. (Psalm 46:7)

In the storms of life, help us know Your presence, Lord, and to share Your goodness and mercy with others.

In a Word...

Thanks. Wonderful! Good job!

Whatever your age or stage in life, positive reinforcement never goes out of style. Psychologist Maryann Troiani says there's more to this than ego-stroking: "Negative words sap our enthusiasm; inspirational words boost your mood and motivate you."

Troiani suggests that there are certain words that can instantly improve your state of mind and uplift you any day of the week. They include:

Begin: Take charge by finally starting that long-postponed project. "You will become energized," says Troiani.

Imagine: Your imagination has no boundaries. Says one woman, "Dreaming about something is the first step toward achievement."

Believe: Tell yourself you will succeed, and you'll set your mind and attitude in the right direction.

Look for ways to encourage yourself and those around you to live life wisely, well and to the fullest!

Prosper for us the work of our hands—O prosper the work of our hands! (Psalm 90:17)

Help me maintain edifying, positive thoughts, Jesus.

He Makes Sure You Hear the Words

In a business world ruled by ink jet and laser printers, Paul Schweitzer can hold his own. But in the world of manual typewriters, this 67-year-old businessman is king.

"Dinosaurs" is how Schweitzer lovingly refers to the black, gray, olive and red typewriters that fill his office in Manhattan's Flatiron Building.

"Some writers still like to hear their words hit the page," Schweitzer says.

Gramercy Typewriter Company was opened in 1932 by his father Abraham. Paul Schweitzer, then 18, went to work learning how to fix typewriter carriages and change ribbons. Today, he continues, even making "office calls" with a black leather kit that resembles a medical bag. He repairs computer printers as well.

Modern ways can make life easier. But there are always some things in life that stand the test of time. Choose well from the best of the old and the new.

The wisdom of the scribe depends on leisure. (Sirach 38:24)

Eternal Lord, Your love for us remains the same, yesterday, today and forever.

Throw Yourself into Your Work

If you had served your country as well as a renowned statesman, general and tactician, you would probably expect to be rewarded with better position than garbage collector.

But in ancient Greece that's just what happened to Epaminondes. His enemies wanted to humble him and had him put in charge of sanitation for Thebes, his home city. But the great leader threw himself into the daunting task, saying, "If the position will not reflect glory on me, I will reflect glory on the work."

He succeeded brilliantly—and to the acclaim of all in Greece.

We don't get to choose every situation that happens in our lives, but we always have the opportunity to choose our own attitude. Never be afraid to live life with as much enthusiasm—and good judgment—as possible.

See, I am sending you out like sheep into the midst of wolves; so be wise as serpents and innocent as doves. (Matthew 10:16)

You have given me a mission, Holy God, which You have given to no other. Inspire me to fulfill it with all my will and all my strength—for love of You.

Turning the Pages in Life Stories

When numerous immigrants from Latin America and Asia moved into Mary Fischer's Los Angeles, California, neighborhood, she convinced herself that she had nothing in common with them.

"I fortressed myself in my house and rarely spoke to any of them," she said. Then, Fischer suffered two major losses: her six-figure job as a senior writer for a national magazine and her relationship with a man she loved both ended.

These events pushed her to connect with her neighbors and to learn more about them. "I discovered how extraordinary they were," she said. "I see now how their lives and mine include experiences universal to us all: loss, disappointment, hope and love."

Choosing not to connect with people before we know anything about them is like deciding against a book before reading even one page. In life, as with literature, then, let the adventure begin!

You shall not wrong or oppress a resident alien. (Exodus 22:21)

Today and every day, Master, help me to show reverence for Your presence in each person.

Animals' Migrations

Many animals change habitats with the changing seasons. But where do they go? And how do they get there? Consider these animals' fascinating annual journeys, for example:

Whales–Guided by magnetite in their brains which functions as a magnetic compass, whales move from sub polar to subtropical seas to reproduce.

Spiny Lobsters–Each year these clawless relatives of crayfish migrate en masse, single-file across the ocean floor. They use the earth's magnetic field for guidance. Experts believe this migration is linked to reproduction.

Turtles–Each year, thousands of female green turtles swim more than 1,000 miles across the Atlantic Ocean from Brazil to Ascension Island where they dig shallow nests and deposit their leathery eggs. Then they swim back to Brazil!

There are more marvels in God's creation than the human mind can fathom. All the more reason not to despoil, but to cherish and preserve Earth and Earth's creatures.

They will not hurt or destroy on all My holy mountain. (Isaiah 11:9)

Fill me with wonder at the mystery and majesty of Your creatures, Creator.

She Had a Dream

For decades Joan Maynard worked to preserve Weeksville, a 19th-century African-American community in Brooklyn, New York. It's now on the National Register of Historic Places.

Weeksville was home to the first African-American woman physician in New York State, the city's first black policeman, as well as *The Freedman's Torchlight,* one of the U.S.'s first black newspapers.

Were it not for Maynard this history would have remained lost. But she felt it important for people, especially youth, to know and take pride in their history.

After Maynard's death, Pamela Green, Maynard's successor as executive director of the Society for the Preservation of Weeksville, acknowledged her "perseverance, her persistence, her beliefs, her strength and her courage."

How will you be remembered?

The memory of the righteous is a blessing. (Proverbs 10:7)

Remind us, Merciful Savior, that it's important to preserve not only historical towns and buildings, but also the memory and stories of people.

Helping Out Helps

People from New Orleans and the Gulf Coast made homeless by Hurricane Katrina sought refuge in many places. One of them was Shepherd's Inn, a facility that normally shelters a few families visiting loved ones at a prison near Port Arthur, Texas.

The Inn opened its doors to 175 men, women and children who had evacuated after the storm. Despite the hardship they had endured, they wanted to show their appreciation. Mary Green, the resident manager, said that "one by one our new residents asked the same question, 'How can I help?'"

A chef and a nutritionist became cooks, a contractor made repairs. Even the youngsters pitched in. And as the guests worked, they talked–and that helped them deal with their loss. They have moved on now, but they left Shepherd's Inn in better shape than it was in before.

Whatever grief we endure, helping others will help us, too.

Do not forget a friend during the battle. (Sirach 37:6)

Holy Lord, show me the way to reach out to those who need my help.

Keeping the Fun in Games

Sara Simpson was reprimanded for giggling during a break in basketball practice. "Laugh someplace else," the coach told the 10-year-old. Not long after that, the girl quit the team.

Across the country, many children are rejecting sports because adults are draining all the fun out of it, explains Fred Engh, president of the National Alliance for Youth Sports and author of *Why Johnny Hates Sports.*

Kids are dropping out because of burnout; an emphasis on competition; and a lack of enjoyment.

But some parents, like Brooke de Lench of Concord, Massachusetts, are bucking the trend. Upset that her sons were rejected by an over-the-top coach, she started her own soccer team and even established a web site to advise parents and youngsters about sports and related issues.

Adult life brims over with more than enough competition and stress. Kids should be allowed to play so that they can have fun and develop their skills. Encourage them.

The streets of the city shall be full of boys and girls playing in its streets. (Zechariah 8:5)

Child Jesus, watch over girls and boys at play.

The Teacher Who Couldn't Retire

After 25 years teaching fifth grade in Gas City, Indiana, Joan Futrell retired – for a while.

Bored, she tried a few other jobs. Finally, she says, "I knew the Lord was letting me know teaching was where I was supposed to be." More than that, she realized that it was the difficult students, the misfits whom she wanted to help.

So Futrell used her pension and Social Security benefits to start an alternate school which she named the Aslan Learning Center. Her first two students were a 14-year-old who had been expelled and a teen mother. In the ten years since then, she's taught scores of young people reading, social studies, science, math and English. She also teaches the Ten Commandments and the Twenty-third Psalm.

"The best part is getting a hug," says the definitely non-retired teacher. "That hug is worth all the work."

Someone needs what each of us has to give – ourselves.

Teach me Your way, O Lord. (Psalm 27:11)

Beloved Lord, show me how to reach out to those who could benefit from the talents You have given.

Ways Not to Worry about Health Care Costs

Good health is priceless. Here are some ideas to help you achieve it without spending a fortune:

Wash your hands often. Soap and water are your best weapons against flu and colds.

Take a daily walk. Walking works off extra calories – and builds up vitamin D from sunlight.

Write it down. Expressing your feelings in a journal can help get things off your chest and may improve health problems.

Get enough rest. Skimping on sleep saps your energy, compromises your immune system and can play a role in developing diabetes, hypertension and obesity.

Chill out. Finding ways to lower your stress can strengthen your resistance to illness.

Be sociable. Spend time with people who make you feel more alive, happy and optimistic.

In your choices for your health and for life in general, be good to yourself – true to the special person God made and loves.

There is no wealth better than health of body and no gladness above joy of heart. (Sirach 30:16)

Divine Physician, bless doctors and all health care professionals.

Our Creator's Children

"Ignorance is not bliss," believes a Muslim teen who's a member of the Milwaukee Area Interfaith Youth Forum. They are trying to replace ignorance with knowledge and respect.

Founded after the September 11th attacks, 18 Jewish, Catholic and Muslim young people came together along with adult leaders in an effort to increase understanding, reduce misinformation and promote peace. The group has grown and has sponsored a number of events that help the teens learn about each other–and their beliefs.

One Jewish teen said that at such gatherings it's easy to take it for granted that people of different faiths can get along. "But you know that's not the case in many parts of the world," he said. "We are here so that our children don't have to grow up in a world as violent as ours and with as much hatred as ours."

Do all you can to build peace each and every day.

A harvest of righteousness is sown in peace for those who make peace. (James 3:18)

Creator of all, help us love Your children, our sisters and brothers, with both courtesy and courage.

From a Mournful Day, a Promising Career

New York City police officer Daniel Rodriguez gained notice when he sang "The Star Spangled Banner" at New York Yankees games after September 11, 2001. His clear and haunting voice provoked comparisons between him and the late Mario Lanza.

Although Rodriguez's debut was salted with sadness, it launched a promising career. Since leaving the police department to concentrate on his singing, he's had the chance to study with tenor Placido Domingo and to team with Lea Salonga of *Miss Saigon* fame on a bi-lingual album of sacred and spiritual songs titled *In the Presence*.

"My life has always been based on my faith," Rodriguez says. "My life has always been a series of coincidences and having the faith to say, 'This is where I'm supposed to be.'"

Each of us needs to determine where God wants us to be and what God wants us to do. Ask Him to deepen your faith.

"I believe; help my unbelief!" (Mark 9:24)

Abba, give me faith enough to persevere in hard times.

Pray Today, Pray Everyday

For most of us, learning to pray is a lifetime process, one that benefits from daily efforts.

Rabbi Abraham Joshua Heschel offered these thoughts on the value of persistence in prayer:

"Prayer is not a stratagem for occasional use, a refuge to resort to now and then. It is rather like an established residence for the innermost self. All things have a home; the bird has a nest, the fox has a hole, the bee has a hive. A soul without prayer is a soul without a home. ...To pray is to open a door where both God and the soul may enter."

Remember, too, that your union with God depends more on His love for you than on your love for Him. God desires you. God unites Himself with you. Rest in God's love.

Pray without ceasing. (1 Thessalonians 5:17)

Guide me, Spirit of God, that I may learn to rest and rejoice in Your presence.

Baking a Difference

When Michael Gualano saw scenes of the destruction after Hurricane Katrina, he wanted to do something for the affected people. "I felt bad for them," he said.

The nine-year-old from Mamaroneck, New York, got busy—and got baking. A fifth grader who wants to become a chef, he spent two days making brownies, cookies and other treats. His mom helped him with the "oven part" and with cutting. "He wouldn't let me do anything else," she said.

Michael even got his grandmother to make madeleines and a local bakery to donate cupcakes.

Then he held a bake sale. And when his five-hour Saturday bake sale ended, he had $387 to send to the American Red Cross.

"I felt happy that I was helping someone," said Michael.

Indeed, the smallest deed, done with great love, can make a big difference for others—and for how we see ourselves.

Truly I tell you, unless you change and become like children, you will never enter the kingdom of heaven. (Matthew 18:3)

Enable us to be generous, Jesus, that we may reach out with love to our sisters and brothers in need.

Fulfilling Potential and Doing Good

How did one immigrant woman fulfill her potential?

Born in El Cambio, Mexico, to an American citizen father, Antonia Hernandez, her six younger siblings and her parents came to the U.S. in 1956 for better educational opportunities. While working to help support herself and her family, Hernandez earned her law degree from UCLA in 1974.

Wanting to protect the civil rights of Latinos, Hernandez spent years working to insure their participation in the electoral process. The long time activist is now president of the California Community Foundation, one of the largest community foundations in the country, which helps people in need by funding health, education and other projects.

Antonia Hernandez wants "every person to have the opportunity to fulfill his or her potential. ...We're creating a community in which we're all interdependent. It's what makes this country so great."

Strive to fulfill your own potential.

Deborah, a prophetess...was judging Israel... and the Israelites came up to her for judgment. (Judges 4:4,5)

Holy Trinity, unite us in our efforts for justice and mercy.

Giving a Helping Hand

At a young age, Patrick Taylor realized that he would have to work hard in order to get far in life. He left home at the age of 16, put himself through college, and became a self-made Louisiana oilman.

Years later, while on a visit to a local middle school, Taylor met students from a troubled area of New Orleans. Having faced his own difficulties growing up, he decided to make them a deal. He promised to finance their college education if they maintained solid B's throughout high school.

Since that initial school visit in 1988, Taylor has bankrolled more than 500 students spending approximately $300,000 a year financing scholarships.

He insists that all kids can overcome difficulties and accomplish great things if they believe in their potential.

Believing in our God-given potential is vital—but so is giving our best to help others.

**A generous person has cause to rejoice.
(Sirach 40:14)**

Remind us to use our resources well for the benefit of Your children in need, Generous Lord.

What Can I Do?

"What can I do?" can sound hopeless, as if to say the problem is way too big and nothing can be done.

But asked another way, as did Debbie and David Alexander, it's a call to action. Let me do whatever I can, however small or insignificant it may seem.

After meeting a group of young singers from an orphanage in war-torn Liberia on tour in the U.S., the Alexanders first adopted two of the orphans and, later, their siblings.

It wasn't easy. As the biological mother of two college aged sons, Debbie Alexander didn't know if she was prepared to return to the rigors of parenting young teens. The couple faced problems they never anticipated, but their rewards have been tremendous.

Caring for the world's orphaned children is a huge undertaking. Yet all we need do is our small part.

Father of orphans and protector of widows is God in His holy habitation. (Psalm 68:5)

War, famine, poverty, disease, lack of maternal health care—these and other problems cause children to be orphaned. Father, show us how to save Your children.

Activist's Balancing Act

Pharmacist Yasser Maisari was torn between his desire to spend more time with his family and his need to right a wrong.

Someone had to control the noise and air pollution created by Dearborn's industrial plants. Despite important family commitments, he knew he couldn't look the other way: he would speak up at local meetings.

"We know we're going up against big business," said Maisari. "But it gets depressing when city officials and people who are supposed to represent the community either ignore you or tell you to move."

Maisari and his neighbors celebrated success when they won a class-action lawsuit.

Yet the fight for a cleaner environment continues across this country. There will always be a need for citizens to be involved; to juggle familial and community responsibilities.

The balancing act isn't an easy one. But it is important.

Do not hate hard labor. (Sirach 7:15)

Teach us how to be good citizens and loving members of our families, Blessed Trinity.

Defying Expectations

Everyone knows institutional food is terrible. No college student happily eats at the campus cafeteria.

Tell that to students trying to sneak into the dining hall at Yale University's Berkeley College. As reported by *The New York Times*, "Non-Berkeley students try to sneak in the back door...try to slip fake identification cards past the Yale employees stationed at the entrance. They don (Berkeley) sweatshirts..."

The reason is the Sustainable Food Project which was started to support area farmers and promote healthier eating. Only a relatively few students can legitimately eat in this dining hall where the food is fresh, organic, mostly locally grown (including in the student garden) and also delicious.

It's not just institutional food that, often rightly, is pigeonholed. Are you, rightly or wrongly, pigeonholed? Defy expectations, be who God made you to be.

The truth will make you free. (John 8:32)

The pressure to conform is almost irresistible, Abba. Strengthen and encourage each one of us so we may be the persons You created us to be moment by moment.

Teachers with Baby Faces

Mary Gordon is a miracle worker, of sorts. She improves children's educational performance, reduces in-school aggression, helps teens avoid parenthood while preparing them to be caring parents in the future, and, as one judge claims, reduces crime.

And she does this by making sure that elementary school classrooms get a 30-minute visit once a month–from a baby.

Since Gordon founded her program, Roots of Empathy, five years ago, she has reached 65,000 students between age three and 14 in more than 2,500 Canadian classrooms. Under an instructor's leadership classroom discussions are about the feelings and trials of growing up, and about parent-child relationships.

"I'm convinced that a peaceful world begins with children," Gordon explains. "This type of direct encounter appears to have an enormously positive impact."

From our first breath, we have a job that only we can do–gifts that only we can offer.

Blessed are the peacemakers, for they will be called children of God. (Matthew 5:9)

Creator, You gave us life and You sustain it. Fill us with Your spirit so that we may serve and strengthen others.

After Breaking–Wholeness

While grieving the loss of both her mother and grandmother, Elissa Montanti read a letter from a teenage boy named Kenan Malkic who lost his arms and legs to a landmine during the Bosnian civil war. Touched by his note, she felt a voice within urging her to do something.

Montanti raised enough funds to bring Malkic to the United States to have surgery, and has since helped over 40 other children who have endured similar losses. She now heads Global Medical Relief Fund, a non-profit group that arranges for free surgery, treatment and prostheses for other children like him.

Elissa Montanti took her emotional pain and used it to benefit others. When asked how she changed his life, Kenan Malkic said, "She made me feel whole."

Each of us experience situations where our lives feel broken. By picking up the pieces for one another, we can all become whole.

Tell John...the blind receive their sight, the lame walk, the lepers are cleansed, the deaf hear, the dead are raised, the poor have good news brought to them. (Luke 7:22)

Help us, Merciful Jesus, to care for each other in our mutual brokenness.

About Yom Kippur

Yom Kippur, the holiest day in the Jewish year, is also known as the Day of Atonement. Writing in *America* about it, Rabbi Michael Lerner says that "our fundamental inclination...is toward the good: but...we miss the mark." He adds, "We take collective responsibility" because "we co-create our world."

Rabbi Lerner suggests that as individuals and as a nation we examine our attitudes and obligations toward today's major world problems. What do we really think about:

- International efforts to reduce global warming
- Extremes of poverty, both domestic and international
- Health care coverage for all
- True respect and practical support for parents and children

What would our country and world be like if we lived righteousness and love?

Have mercy on me, O God according to your steadfast love...Wash me thoroughly from my iniquity. (Psalm 51:1,2)

Holy Spirit, enable us to express our goodness through our deeds.

Jump-Starting the Day for First Graders

Most weekday mornings, if you walk by a certain first-grade class room in Salisbury, North Carolina, don't be surprised if you hear kids shouting and see them jumping around.

The students are not out of control. They're participating in an aerobics class with volunteer class mom Jennifer Burks.

A registered nurse and aerobics instructor, Burks became alarmed at childhood obesity statistics and the lack of exercise and movement in youngsters' daily lives. Her solution: offer a 30-40 minute session to her daughter's classmates each week to help them get moving and exercising. "These kids need to be taught how to live a healthy lifestyle," she says.

Jennifer Burks gives of her time and expertise to help address a widespread problem.

While we can't solve all the world's problems, we can make a difference in the lives of a few people—or even just one.

Love one another with mutual affection; outdo one another in showing honor. (Romans 12:10)

Remind me that if we each helped just one person our world would be a better place, Creator.

Wrong Room, Right Moves

In 1984, Gretchen Buchenholz was on her way to a government office for a day-care permit when, by accident, she entered a room where homeless families were waiting to be placed in a "welfare hotel."

She saw three bare cribs with babies in them. The children wore no diapers–their parents couldn't afford them. The room was filthy.

Buchenholz forgot the permit, marched out of the room, and returned with bread, peanut butter, apple juice and diapers. Then she started making telephone calls, ultimately helping to set up transitional housing for those families and, since then, many homeless families like them.

More than two decades later, Buchenholz, as founder of the Association to Benefit Children, continues to make a difference for homeless families.

Be alert to ways in which you can help helpless infants and children.

As you did to one of the least of these who are member of My family, you did it to Me. (Matthew 25:40)

Gentle Jesus, how may I best show others Your compassionate, loving kindness?

A Welcome Letter

During her freshman year at Minnesota's University of St. Thomas, Amanda Reding received a mysterious letter of encouragement signed by "Barnabas."

Amanda wasn't the first to receive a message from "Barnabas." For the past ten years, the inspirational pen pal has been sending modest amounts of money and words of enlightenment to college-bound members of the United Methodist Church in Rosemount.

"Barnabas" is actually a 39-year-old father of two who, while himself in college, received encouraging notes from a family friend. Realizing that this is the first time many students are on their own, he signs his letters using the name of the apostle who offered advice to St. Paul. Barnabas says "I want to help them maintain a connection," and let them know that they are not alone.

It's important to remember that we are never alone.

The Lord God...will feed His flock like a shepherd; He will gather the lambs in His arms, and carry them in His bosom, and gently lead the mother sheep. (Isaiah 40:10,11)

Good Shepherd, gather infants, children, teens and young adults within Your sheepfold. Protect them. Cherish them.

Winnebago-ing Through Life

When some people say they're making a fresh start, you may want to take them seriously.

Marilyn Abraham, for example, woke up one morning in 1995 and decided she needed to change her life. After 22 years as a high-powered Manhattan book editor, she realized that her life and happiness were more important than furthering her already impressive corporate career.

Abraham and her husband, Sandy, took an Alaskan road trip. They were exhilarated by being on the open road amidst the most beautiful scenery and nature they'd ever seen.

As a result, they quit their jobs, made their plans and eventually bought a Winnebago mobile home. Now they write, travel, teach and manage their finances carefully so they can remain un-tethered to corporate jobs.

Freedom's price is responsibility. Do you appreciate your own freedom and that of others?

I am responsible for the lives of all.
(1 Samuel 22:22)

God, remind us that we are each responsible for the preservation of each others' freedoms.

Triumph Over Failure

A banquet was held in England many years ago to honor Sir Edmund Mallory who, together with others in his party, had died during their third attempt to climb Mount Everest in 1924.

The senior member of the survivors stood up at the banquet and turned to face a huge picture of Mallory. He is quoted as saying, through his tears, "I speak to you, Mount Everest, in the name of all brave men living and those yet unborn. Mount Everest you defeated us once, you defeated us twice, you defeated us three times.

"But Mount Everest, we shall someday defeat you, because you can't get any bigger and we can!"

Defeat need not defeat us. Even through tears, keep learning, growing, improving.

We beseech You, give us success! (Psalm 118:25)

Keep me resolutely hopeful in the face of defeat, Jesus.

In the Story Booth

One person recalls the birth of a baby on a subway train. A man from India speaks of his initial confusion at seeing "hot dog" on an American menu. A mother tells of her family's persecution by the Nazis.

These stories are some of the hundreds collected by StoryCorps, an oral history project that encourages people to describe their life experiences. The tiny recording studio is located in New York City's Grand Central Terminal.

David Isay, a radio producer, created the project to put traditional oral history in the hands of "regular" people instead of academics and journalists.

"You can bring anyone you choose," Isay explains, "and conduct a 40-minute oral history interview with the help of a facilitator." One multiple tale-teller says, "Every time I go I feel lit from within."

Each person's life stories are worth sharing, especially for the lessons to be learned.

**Remember me, O my God, for good.
(Nehemiah 13:31)**

The greatest story ever told is that of Your limitless love for us, Lord God. May we reflect that love in our lives!

Taking on the State of California

Sweetie Williams' son, Eliezer, told him that he didn't have homework because there weren't enough books at his San Francisco school. Bathrooms were flooded; ceiling tiles dangled; vermin-infested classrooms were neither cooled nor heated. "Our children are being deprived of opportunity," said Williams, an American Samoan.

The ACLU filed a class-action lawsuit against the state of California with Eliezer Williams as the lead plaintiff. After four years, the state settled the suit, agreeing to spend $188 million to buy books and make repairs in the lowest-performing schools. A system for students, teachers and parents to lodge complaints has been established.

Eliezer Williams believes that he's been taught an important lesson. "I learned that anyone can do this," he says. "Anyone can make a change."

Be willing to stand up not only for your rights, but also for the rights of your neighbors.

We will all stand before the judgement seat of God. (Romans 14:10)

Bless the efforts of those who work to end bias in employment, education, medical care and housing, Creator.

Words That Matter

Imagine. Laugh. Pray. Read. Write. Play. These are just a few of the words that can instantly inspire, improve your frame of mind, and enhance your energy.

The imagination is boundless. *Imagining* something is the first step toward achieving it. *Laughing* broadens one's perspective and makes an unbearable situation easier to cope with.

Praying anywhere and anytime reconnects you with God. *Reading* removes barriers and provides insight into things one may have never considered before. *Writing* gives you a power and freedom that can never be taken away, so try writing in a notebook or journal everyday.

As adults, there is always something that needs to be done, but allow your inner child to come out to *play* every once in a while.

You'll be amazed at the effect these simple activities can have on your life.

Unless you change and become like children, you will never enter the kingdom of heaven. (Matthew 18:3)

Lord, make me a channel of Your faith, hope and love.

The Wisdom of Autumn

Every season and every age has its own special rewards.

Lin Yutang, a Chinese writer and scholar who introduced the literature of his native country to the West, had this to say about autumn and about life:

"I like spring, but it is too young. I like summer but it is too proud. So I like best of all autumn, because its leaves are a little yellow, its tone a little mellower, its colors richer, and it is tinged a little with sorrow.

"Its golden richness speaks not of the innocence of spring, nor of the power of summer, but the mellowness and kindly wisdom of approaching age. It knows the limitations of life and is content."

We need to recognize life's limitations, particularly our own. That doesn't mean that we neglect to do our best. On the contrary, it means gaining a clearer understanding of what God expects us to do with the time He entrusts to us.

Those who live many years should rejoice in them all. (Ecclesiastes 11:8)

Enable me to enjoy time in all its seasons and life in all its ages, Spirit of Wisdom. And to use them well.

Passing the Baton

The KIPP (Knowledge is Power Program) Academy String and Rhythm Orchestra in the Bronx, an outstanding youth orchestra, has toured nationally and performed at Carnegie Hall.

Being involved with this orchestra changes lives in positive ways. Through daily hour-long music class and long rehearsals weekday afternoons and Saturday mornings youngsters learn the value of practice, perseverance and discipline. Many also dream of a life beyond poverty, drugs and violence.

"Playing the violin helped with the stress. And then going on field trips I saw this is what I want. I could see that there are things I can do," said student Lucy Mendoza.

"My job is to make children feel successful. I do that through music," says Jesus Concepción conductor and former student member. The orchestra's founder, Charlie Randall says, "this music is the way out" of anger and hopelessness.

Help a child out of anger and hopelessness.

(Jesus) took a little child and put it among them; and taking it in His arms, He said to them, "Whoever welcomes one such child in My name welcomes Me." (Mark 9:36-37)

Remind us, Jesus, that children are of infinite value.

Sisters in Faith

When Rita Chiavacci's son Michael was killed by a drunk driver, she fought to keep her grief from turning into despair. She held fast to her faith in God–and turned to doll making to occupy her hands and heart. Her doll creations proved popular, resulting in a booming business.

Two decades later, Chiavacci met Valerie Rambach. The two were opposites in many ways: Chiavacci was Catholic; Rambach, Jewish. Chiavacci was married, while Rambach had remained single, caring for her elderly mother while working as an X-ray technician. Yet a strong friendship developed.

When Rambach's mother died, Chiavacci supported her friend, even inviting her to come and stay with her and her husband. Rambach turned out to be a fine doll maker as well.

"We like to say we are truly soul sisters," says Rambach.

Faith lived out in love of neighbor can bring light to the darkest of times.

Faith by itself, if it has no works, is dead. (James 2:17)

Redeemer, send me Your love.

Abundant Life in a Valley Called Death

When some people think of Death Valley National Park, they think of an oppressively hot, arid desert that can barely support any life.

While it's true that Death Valley typically receives no more than two inches of rain annually, in 2005 the area got more than six. Visitors to the park, particularly those who traveled off the beaten path, had a glorious surprise.

The abundant rainfall caused dormant seeds to germinate into exquisite purple, yellow and other boldly colored desert flowers. The chia, for example, has delicate tiny orchid-like flowers which unfold from a pointed purple sphere–hardly a flower one would expect in Death Valley!

Life and beauty are everywhere on God's good earth. The most unlikely places reveal the most stunning beauty. Conserve earth's loveliness.

Like a cedar...a cypress...a palm tree...like rose-bushes in Jericho; like a fair olive tree...a plane tree...I spread out my branches.
(Sirach 24:13,14,16)

Eternal God, help me delight in the subtle beauty and tenacious life of Your trees, shrubs and flowers.

Beyond Borders

Leader. Humanitarian. French politician. Iconoclast. Co-founder of Medecins sans Frontieres (Doctors Without Borders). Those words describe Bernard Kouchner.

Time magazine said that he had sworn "to banish forever the kind of error made by the Red Cross from 1940 to 1944, when it distributed packages, but remained silent over the crime of the death camps, where his grandparents perished."

So whether it's Vietnam, Somalia, Biafra or elsewhere, Kouchner doesn't just bring medicine, he witnesses to the suffering and violence. "I ran to Biafra, because I was too young for Guernica, Auschwitz, Oradour and Settiff."

Nelson Mandela once said to Kouchner "Thanks for intervening in matters that don't concern you."

As poet John Donne said, "no man is an island, entire of itself...any man's death diminishes me, because I am involved in mankind."

My eyes flow with rivers of tears because of the destruction of my people. (Lamentations 3:48)

Merciful Savior, give us hearts like Yours— overflowing with compassionate action on behalf of our suffering and oppressed sisters and brothers.

Hero on a Street Corner

New York businesswoman Regina Farage was headed to dinner with a friend, when a self-sacrificing decision saved the life of a toddler.

Farage noticed a toddler standing in the middle of a two-way Brooklyn street, directly in the line of oncoming traffic. Frantically she shouted a warning to the child, but he didn't budge.

She jumped out of her car, ran to the boy and got him out of the way, but she herself was hit by a car. She sustained a broken hip and injuries to her knees and neck.

Still on crutches more than two months after saving the youngster's life and "in pain every day," Farage had no regrets. She told reporters, "I would never have lived with myself to know that a little boy could have died."

Heroism requires sacrifice. Let doing the right thing be its own reward.

He went down with them...to Nazareth, and was obedient to them. ...And Jesus increased in wisdom and in years, and in divine and human favor. (Luke 2:51,52)

Jesus, help us live Your kind of moment-by-moment, quiet, noble and life-affirming heroism.

This Little Life

To Steve and Heather Gemmens rape was a word they'd heard on the six o'clock news from time to time. They never imagined it would become part of their lives, ever.

So when Heather was raped and became pregnant as a result, the couple feared they'd never recover. At first, they were completely overwhelmed.

As time passed, Heather realized she couldn't part with the baby through adoption. "How can I give away this little life stirring inside me?"

Today, their daughter Rachel is thriving. While the crime of rape changed their lives forever, they believe the path they chose helped bring a positive end to a violent crime.

Rape and all crimes of violence diminish our God-given humanity. Strive to make peace and respect part of your life—and our world.

Put away violence and oppression.
(Ezekiel 45:9)

Loving Father, protect the rights and physical integrity of women and girls, men and boys. Help us respect one another.

From the Many...Riches

When Columbus made landfall on Hispanola and later the Pilgrims on Cape Cod, they found vibrant Native American nations with complex languages. Here are a few words from these Native American languages which have enriched American English.

- bayou – Choctaw "bayuk"
- chipmunk – Ojibwa "ajidamoon"
- kayak – Alaskan Yupik "qayaq"
- moose – Eastern Abenaki "mos"
- pecan – Illinois "pakani"
- squash – Narragansett "askutasquash"
- Kentucky – Iroquoi "Kentahten" for "land of tomorrow"
- (Lake) Tahoe – Washo "tahoe" for "big water"

The United States is in every way the richer for being a nation of Native Americans, immigrants and descendants of immigrants from the rest of the world. Appreciate its past and work for its future.

You know the heart of an alien, for you were aliens in the land of Egypt. (Exodus 23:9)

Help us celebrate and maintain the rich diversity of this land, Creator of all.

Live by Your Own Values

Kelly Underwood, 23-years-old, rented a PG-13 movie using a gift certificate. Given the rating, she thought it would be a generally family-friendly flick. But after only 10 minutes she turned it off and returned it. "She knew it was not something I would approve of," said Kelly's mom.

Meanwhile, a Dove Foundation study showed that G-rated films were 11 times more profitable than R-rated films. Yet, Hollywood produces 12 times more R-rated films than G-rated ones.

Fortunately, these statistics are making an impact. Hollywood execs are finally realizing that families are fed up with violence and sleaze and that they will pay for what they want.

Create change through your wallet. Patronize vendors, products and services that meet your personal non-violent values. Avoid the others. And let industry leaders know what you support–and what you don't.

The wise of heart is called perceptive.
(Proverbs 16:21)

Holy God, help us act according to our beliefs.

Paying the Price for "Liquid Gold"

Crude oil, once called "liquid gold," has again earned that moniker. Prices at the gas pump or for heating oil give new meaning to the word "expensive."

These times call for more trustworthy stewardship of God's gifts so as to reduce the demand for "liquid gold" as well as coal and natural gas. Here are some suggestions:

- Don't buy "gas guzzlers" at the auto dealership.
- Wash clothes in cold or warm water, not hot.
- Use a programmable thermostat to heat and cool your home.
- Clean or replace air filters regularly.
- Caulk and weather strip doors, windows; insulate attics.
- Recycle and/or reuse paper, fabrics, metal, glass and plastics.
- Compost food scraps; avoid oil-based fertilizers.
- Walk, bike, carpool or use public transit.

Use all natural resources wisely.

It is required of stewards that they be found trustworthy. (1 Corinthians 4:2)

Remind us that by conserving what's Yours, Holy Spirit, we honor You.

A Bag of Calm

Loretta Kush wanted to keep her best friend calm. Kush knew that while her friend's husband was going through a lengthy surgery, her pal would be nervously pacing the waiting room. Worry was inevitable. There had to be something Kush could do.

Finally she decided–and packed a pretty tote bag for her friend. Inside it were helpful goodies such as bottled water, snacks, hand sanitizer, tissues, aspirin, a pen and a crossword puzzle book.

Not only did Kush's friend appreciate the thoughtful gift, but so did everyone in the waiting room to whom she showed the bag.

Our loving actions directed to one person can bring help and hope to others as well. The joy of a good deed is contagious!

The good person out the good treasure of the heart produces good. (Luke 6:45)

Show me a quiet place within, my Savior, where I can offer You thanks and praise.

Life-Giving Waters

It's easy to take potable water, a precious resource, for granted if you live where water is abundant.

But there are all-too-many areas where water is as much a luxury as it is a necessity—and, its presence is cause for celebration.

For instance, there was a festive dedication ceremony with 3,000 people in attendance when a major collaborative effort brought a water system to the residents of 14 communities in the state of Olancho, Honduras. For the first time in their lives they had running water available. Contributions were made in money, support and physical labor by various Catholic agencies, the European Union and the Honduran government.

If water gushes from your home's faucets, appreciate how valuable that is, how rare for most of the world's people. Then, decide to conserve it.

Jesus said to her, "...those who drink of the water that I will give them will never be thirsty....(it) will become in them a spring of water gushing up to eternal life. (John 4:13,14)

Lead "me beside still waters," Good Shepherd.

Understanding Islam

Christians, Jews and Muslims share a common belief in the same one God. But what else should we know about Islam?

In the early 7th century, Mohammed, a merchant, had a mystical experience. Muslims believe that through the Angel Gabriel, he had a series of revelations which became the Koran. They revere this as the Word of God.

The Five Pillars of Islam consist of, first, a profession of faith–"There is no god but Allah, and Mohammed is the prophet of Allah." Second, prayers are said five times a day. Next, almsgiving: Muslims traditionally give 2.5 percent of their wealth to the poor. Fourth is Ramadan, when Muslims fast from sunrise to sunset during this holy month. Finally, a pilgrimage, or hajj to Mecca, Mohammed's birthplace, is expected of Muslims, if possible.

We all have so much to learn. Let's remember that half of communication is listening.

God said to (Abram)...No longer shall your name be Abram, but your name shall be Abraham, for I have made you the ancestor of a multitude of nations. (Genesis 17:3,5)

God of Abraham and Sarah, You treasure all Your children. May we imitate You in love and respect.

The Power of Music

Maybe you've also noticed the way music seems to draw people together. Even though he couldn't quite explain it at the time, Paul Sullivan first felt this power of music when he was a nine-year-old choir member.

Although Sullivan's instrument changed from voice to piano his early experience ignited something that has lasted. "I have performed in venues humble and grand, and I am always struck by the power of music," he says.

"Musicians connect with each other, and with listeners," notes Sullivan who's also a composer. "Listeners form a connection with one another." Then if all's well "the music itself connects us all with something much larger than ourselves."

Some say the power of music is love. When this hard-to-describe force "rises in music, for a few precious minutes, all the isolation, the loneliness, disappears."

Listen to music you like–or try something new. Enjoy!

A ruby seal in a setting of gold is...music. (Sirach 32:5)

Holy Spirit, inspire parents and educators to introduce children to the lifelong pleasures of music.

The Struggle Continues

The story of slavery in this country is one of despair, resilience, and ingenuity as well as hope kept alive.

Slavery destroyed families, dashed the dreams of millions and betrayed the ideals on which the United States was founded.

The television documentary *Slavery and the Making of America* describes how pervasive slavery was throughout this country. Yet there were always people who opposed slavery, even if they wouldn't live to see slavery's demise.

Series producer Dante James notes, "Enslaved people were proactive...pushing the agenda of equality and freedom forward."

Achieving freedom and equality for every man, woman and child is incomplete. The struggle for true liberty for all must continue. Do your part.

Proclaim liberty throughout the land. (Leviticus 25:10)

Jesus, we discriminate by race, gender, religion, and more. Remind us that we are all the Father's children—and to love one another.

School's Best Friend

Miss Siggy walks proudly through the halls of Upstate New York's Pine Bush Elementary School. The school's new "therapist," is a dog and students enjoy her calming "hugableness."

"Some kids can't talk with people about problems," says Alex Luciano, a fourth grader. "Dogs can't laugh or tell other people."

Adds third-grader Ryker Bodo: "When a dog kisses you, they're glad that you told them."

The school's social worker Catherine Ricchetti came up with the idea for having this "golden doodle" (golden retriever and poodle mix) spend time with students. While she's encountered kids with allergies or a fear of dogs, she has witnessed Miss Siggy's transforming power on students with fears and anxieties.

"In this crazy, mixed-up world, if you can find something to make things gentler, you should use it," she says.

That sounds like a great idea for all of us.

Let love be genuine...Love one another with mutual affection. (Romans 12:9,10)

In a gentle touch, a sweet smile, a tender hug, I find Your presence, Lord, and am no longer afraid. Thanks for the caring people and companion animals in my life.

Helping the Homeless

Homelessness persists. Thousands of men, women and children are homeless, hungry and without medical care. Reasons cited include an increase in poverty, the prevalence of low-wage, no-benefit jobs and a decrease in affordable housing.

In Washington D.C. poor people can find help at Charlie's Place which is named for its late founder Rev. Charles Gilcrist of St. Margaret's Episcopal Church. The church's outreach ministry helps with legal assistance, medical care, health and hygiene education, and spiritual enrichment. Haircuts are available twice a month. And there's a weekly writer's workshop.

Volunteer nurse Nel van Beusekom says she's "learned to be grateful for what I have through working at Charlie's Place. I respect how our clients keep going every day, how they struggle to maintain a sense of dignity even when they have no place to live."

Respect God's needy people by helping them.

I was hungry and you gave Me food...a stranger and you welcomed Me...naked and you gave Me clothing...sick and you took care of Me. (Matthew 25:35-36)

Help work for a living wage, affordable housing and medical care for Your people, God.

Women Saving the World

Dolores Buckley jumped at the chance to be part of history.

The Massachusetts native was one of the first of 161,000 to volunteer for the Women's Health Initiative (WHI). This 15-year investigation into the major health problems of women aged 50 to 79 "has changed the course of women's health," explains Dr. Elizabeth Nabel, director of the National Heart, Lung and Blood Institute, which funded the groundbreaking research.

The study also gave many volunteers a renewed zest for their own futures. "I don't see age as an impediment to doing what I want to do," said Gloria Grant of Washington, D.C. "Because of the WHI, we have more reason to celebrate, not just getting older but getting better every year."

Sometimes, older women's health concerns are not taken seriously. In this as in all circumstances, we need to recognize real problems and to treat them honestly.

Deborah, a prophetess, wife of Lappidoth, was judging Israel. (Judges 4:4)

Father, we praise You for the wise, strong, courageous, older women in our lives.

Getting Help with Admissions

Lloyd Thacker is not household name. But to parents and young people in the throes of the college admissions process, he's almost a hero. Through his Education Conservancy, the former high school guidance counselor from Oregon, is trying to calm the near-hysteria often associated with getting into college.

"Instead of strategies and what colleges are looking for, he's talking about educational values and what students should be looking for," says Bob Sweeney, a guidance counselor in Westchester County, New York, who arranged for Thacker to visit to his high school.

Thacker says his strategy is less about prescribing answers and more about building a stage on which questions can be discussed. Says the parent of one high schooler, "It was important to be reminded that college is about education and not about competing with your neighbors."

Solving a problem starts with changing your viewpoint.

God...makes my feet like the feet of a deer, and makes me tread upon the heights. (Habakkuk 3:19)

Spirit of Knowledge, help me always to choose the path that will most reflect Your love.

Just a Leaf!

Leaves are an ideal example of the wonder and perfection of God's creation.

Leaves are broad, bladelike, round, oval, feathery or needle-like in shape. They can range in size from only several millimeters long to up to 60 feet, as in some palm trees.

While most leaves derive their green color from a pigment called chlorophyll, others possess additional pigments that give them a red or purple cast. In temperate regions, some leaves turn bright orange, yellow and even pink in autumn.

Leaves are a source of food for animals (grasses) and human beings (artichoke, cabbage, spinach). Bay, thyme, sage and parsley leaves are used to season food. Leaves also supply pharmaceuticals; oils for the manufacture of perfumes and soaps and for flavorings; dyes; fertilizer; and tannins for curing leather.

Pause. Appreciate the variety and beauty of God's creation all around you.

The earth brought forth...trees of every kind bearing fruit with the seed in it. And God saw that it was good. (Genesis 1:12)

Creator, thank You for Your limitless life-giving love, as revealed in the world's beauty!

Reading and Enjoying the Bible

Not as familiar with the Bible as you'd like to be? St. Jerome wrote that "ignorance of Scripture is ignorance of Christ."

Perhaps you think familiarity with the Bible means "studying" which feels negative. But don't you enjoy a letter or story from a friend or relative?

Or perhaps it seems that the Bible is too big or too complicated for you. Can you read a newspaper? Or follow written directions to, say, assemble a table?

Or perhaps you think you do not have time. Well, here are a few suggestions to help you.

First make a little time, then, simply start to read the Bible, a collection of God's letters, poems and stories. Begin with Isaiah, Hosea, the Psalms, the Song of Solomon, or Proverbs in the Old Testament; and, of course, the Gospels in the New Testament: Matthew, Mark, Luke and John.

Begin or increase your acquaintance with God's letters and stories, the Bible, today. Know Christ Jesus.

All Scripture is inspired by God and is useful for teaching, for reproof, for correction, and for training in righteousness. (2 Timothy 3:16)

Holy Spirit, abide with me, inspire me, encourage me as I improve my acquaintance with the Bible.

Do You Believe In Magic?

In a racially and ethnically divided world of intolerance it can seem magical when dissimilar people get along.

It's real magic that brings disparate people together at Cape Town, South Africa's College of Magic. A multi-racial institution long before it was legal, the school serves as training ground for young magicians.

But the school isn't just teaching tricks. Students develop "a myriad of life skills," says David Gore, who founded it in 1980 and serves as director. Trainees learn patience, discipline and communication skills, along with such amazing feats as levitation and how to make a coin disappear.

If only racism, "ethnic cleansing," class hatred and other forms of bigotry would disappear! Now that would truly be magical.

God created humankind in His image, in the image of God He created them; male and female He created them. (Genesis 1:27)

Dear Father, when You created humankind You saw that what You had created "was very good." Remind us that under the skin we are more alike than different, more siblings than strangers.

Boiling Water for a Neighborhood

Victoria Thornton-Lucas remembers the glory days of her Brooklyn, New York, neighborhood. "Bushwick Avenue was fabulous," she said. "Tree-lined streets, no crime."

Then things changed. Poverty, unemployment and drugs moved in. She saw her neighbors eating out of garbage cans and begging for money; elderly people going without food.

So Thornton-Lucas started cooking rice, chicken and vegetables for hungry neighbors. Her efforts eventually formed a soup kitchen which today feeds more than 2,000 people a month. She also began a food pantry, which distributes 250 to 300 bags of canned and dry goods weekly.

"I'm really in love with what I do," says Thornton-Lucas. "When I help someone, it's like helping myself."

In the face of great need, there is usually some way each of us can make a difference. Sometimes, it's as simple as boiling water.

As you did it to one of the least of these who are members of My family, you did it to Me. (Matthew 25:40)

When I see You in need in the person of my neighbor, Divine Master, may my response be immediate and loving.

Mind Your Manners

Talking in movie theaters; slamming doors; littering; loud cell-phone conversation. Whatever happened to good manners–or do manners even matter anymore?

"A well-mannered person, whether a child or adult, stands out in the crowd and is someone others want to be around," says etiquette expert Letitia Baldrige. "He or she automatically becomes a leader who can inspire and encourage others." Showing good manners, she continues, is the ability to live one's daily life "efficiently and with kindness."

And etiquette is more than merely knowing what fork to use at dinner, or saying "please," "thank you," or "you're welcome." Although you can't go wrong using those "magic words" notes Baldrige.

So please, if you wish to be respected, to be treated respectfully and with kindness, treat others that way.

Do to others as you would have them do to you. (Luke 6:31)

Jesus, it isn't always easy to be courteous. Help me.

Her Decision Made Her a Legend

Nearly 50 years ago a woman made a decision that would change the course of not only her life, but the lives of all who came after her. She said "no" to what was demanded of her by an unjust law. Her name was Rosa McCauley Parks.

In 1955, laws in the American South required the separation of the blacks and whites on buses; in restaurants and in other public accommodations. Parks' arrest and imprisonment for refusing to move from a seat in the white section of a bus to stand in the black section initiated a bus boycott in Montgomery, Alabama, that lasted more than a year. It was organized by Rev. Martin Luther King, Jr.

Parks, who died in October, 2005, at age 92, lived to see her decision help inspire the civil rights movement that changed the nation.

Each of us has a responsibility to stand–or, in some cases, sit–for what is right.

Strength and dignity are her clothing, and...she opens her mouth with wisdom. ...A woman who fears the Lord is to be praised. ...Let her works praise her in the city gates.
(Proverbs 31:25, 26, 30-31)

Dear God, give me the courage to change the things I can.

Heart-Filled Service

Physician's assistant Marc O'Regan, speaking of his service in Pakistan after the devastating October, 2005 earthquake said, "This work feeds my soul." The Californian was there with Operation Heartbeat, a medical-relief effort.

Just a month before, O'Regan had served in the United States in the aftermath of Hurricane Katrina. Shockingly, O'Regan died of a massive heart attack in February, 2006. He had been contemplating a return to the work that "fed his soul," in Pakistan.

"Marc was a bright light of humanity, a fearless soul who really dared to live in service of others," wrote Derek Burnett in a *Reader's Digest* profile.

Each of us has been created to be a light in our world. Our task is to discover how to make God's love known in our unique way. Find your "God-job" today!

Take My yoke upon you, and learn from Me; for...My yoke is easy, and My burden is light. (Matthew 11:29,30)

How can I be a "fearless soul," Messiah?

Make a Difference Day

When people believe they can make a difference and are given the opportunity, there's no stopping them. *USA Weekend* highlighted the ways people around the United States pitched in on Make a Difference Day to help those hurt by recent hurricanes.

- Warren, Ohio–Alden Elementary School students, along with families and neighbors collected backpacks, papers, pens and other school supplies for Gulf Coast youngsters.

- Detroit, Michigan–Girl scout Troop 6434 and the Saving Our Kids organization collected funds for the Humane Society to help stranded and abandoned pets.

- Fremont, California–Chadbourne Elementary School students made thank-you cards to express their appreciation to the Coast Guard for their rescue efforts.

There are many ways you can help those whose lives have been turned upside down by natural and man-made calamities. Make a difference today.

Bear one another's burdens. (Galatians 6:2)

Inspire us to whole-souled caring for those adversely affected by disasters, Holy Spirit.

Influence for the Good

How often have you been influenced by a friend? Or made a decision based on someone else's suggestion?

You are affected by other people, and, in turn, have the power to affect them. Every time you say something that changes another person's point of view, you become an opinion-maker with the power to use your influence for the common good.

Whether you write a letter to the editor of a newspaper to express your ideas on an important issue of the day, or recommend a book or movie to a friend, you are changing things for the better. Perhaps you know a candidate for public office who deserves backing, or a local charity or community group that needs support. Don't be afraid to speak up–in a positive, pleasant way.

God didn't put you on earth to be concerned only with your own needs. The world needs all the good you can share.

The Holy Spirit will teach you...what you ought to say. (Luke 12:12)

Holy Paraclete, guide me in using my intelligence and judgment in the light of Your will for our good.

Innovative Teacher

"Everybody here has a mountain to climb," says Suzanna McNamara, a literacy teacher, referring to the students at Bronx International High School.

McNamara is creating her own curriculum because none exists for teaching English to older students who lack native-language literacy. She says, "Students acquire English when they are forced to use it in an authentic way...to discover the differences and the connections they share."

In addition to three 70-minute literacy classes daily she co-teaches a math class for 24 students, tutors in phonics three times a week before school and works one-on-one with students after school. But McNamara has also learned about her students—"their lives, their countries, and their dreams" and in doing so she feels "a special connection to them."

Teaching is a vital profession in a democracy. Support teachers. Encourage collegians to consider a career in teaching

Teach what is good. (Titus 2:3)

Bless, inspire, protect and refresh teachers, Merciful Redeemer.

Enlisting Help to Fight Hunger

Sending a check for a good cause is fine and important. But sometimes there is a better way to contribute.

Bill Shore, founder of Share Our Strength which aids the poor and hungry, is known for encouraging people to donate their talents. For instance, Shore established the annual *Taste of the Nation* event at which famous chefs and restaurateurs cook for contributors.

People are happy to help. By forming alliances with profit-making businesses, Shore's non-profit organization, has raised millions of dollars for the struggle against hunger.

According to restaurant owner Danny Meyer, Shore "has an extraordinary way not only of connecting people with good opportunities but getting people to do the hard work."

Share money, yes. But share skills, too.

A generous person has cause to rejoice. (Sirach 40:14)

Show us how to share our skills as well as our money, Jesus.

Happy Halloween!

To some, Halloween is seen as Satan's holiday, connected with evil. But for one Ohio college professor, Halloween is about chasing the devil away with laughter and joy.

"The one thing Satan cannot bear is to be a source of laughter," says Anderson Rearick III, writing in *Catholic Digest*. "His pride is undermined by his own knowledge that his infernal rebellion against God is in reality, an absurd farce. Hating laughter, he demands to be taken seriously."

Those worried about Halloween are, in effect, giving the devil his due, according to Rearick. Instead, he advocates celebrating Halloween "with gusto." He recommends embracing one's imaginative side, "becoming for a short time something wonderful and strange. If we give up All Hallows Eve, we lose the delight of God's gift of imagination," he says.

Remember the darkest hour is no match for the light of God's love.

Even the darkness is not dark to you; the night is as bright as the day, for darkness is as light to you. (Psalm 139:12)

Father, deliver me from fear. Keep me safe in Your love.

The Paradox of Love

What is love? A feeling certainly, but also choices and actions–and a focus on the other person. Here are some thoughts on love's meaning:

- Love delights in giving attention rather than in attracting it.
- Love seeks the good in the other person and builds on it rather than magnifying defects.
- Love sees the other person's point of view without necessarily embracing it.
- Love knows how to disagree without becoming disagreeable.
- Love rejoices at others' success instead of being envious.
- Love avoids causing unnecessary pain.
- Love goes out of its way to do something for others without counting the cost.

Love is a flame that warms, but never burns.

Now faith, hope, and love abide, these three; and the greatest of these is love.
(1 Corinthians 13:13)

Remind me, Spirit of Love, that You are the source of all genuine love.

Family Mourns Precious Gift

When three year old Gift Msunzi of Malawi developed acute malaria, he was already debilitated by severe anemia. Named Gift by his father because he believes every child is a gift from God, he died despite the best efforts of his family.

Too often, African children die because they lack access to basic medical care and drugs as well as clean drinking water. And they can't afford simple things like mosquito netting for their beds that could avert disease.

But there are bright spots. Millennium Promise, a philanthropic agency, arranges for private and corporate donors to supply needed cash to local people. Then they can purchase seeds and fertilizer; build a basic medical clinic stocked with drugs; and buy mosquito netting.

The need is urgent. Every life is precious, but more than that, it's a gift from God.

Let the little children come to me...for it is to such as these that the kingdom of God belongs. (Luke 18:16)

Console parents whose children have died, Good Shepherd. And help us save those who still live.

Blind Faith to the Finish Line

One beautiful morning, as part of her training for the New York City Marathon, Nooria Nodrat ran in Central Park.

But on a day filled with color and light, Nodrat saw none of it. She is one of two dozen blind and visually impaired runners participating in the historic race.

Like the others, Nodrat will be tethered via scarf, tie, towel, or bungee cord to a sighted runner who will help her avoid collisions, find toilets and water, and stay upright when well-meaning fellow competitors pat her on the back for encouragement.

Although blind runners develop sound and smell cues that help in the race–and they even learn to "feel" the road with each step–their sighted partner is their lifeline to the finish line.

We can all use a little help on life's journey and can benefit from fresh insight into each day's challenges.

You shall not...put a stumbling block before the blind...I am the Lord. (Leviticus 19:14)

Open my eyes, Divine Creator, so that I more clearly see that all I see reflects Your love.

In Love's Kitchen

Twins Helen Ashe and Ellen Liddell Turner are almost 80 and they've never met a stranger they didn't want to nourish.

For 20 years, the retired nurses have run Love Kitchen, a Knoxville, Tennessee center that serves hot meals to hundreds of needy people each week. In addition, weekly food packages go to 1,500 elderly and handicapped homebound people.

Besides much needed-nourishment, the women provide their own special "ingredient"– nobody walks through the front doors of Love Kitchen without a hug from each. Says one volunteer, "That hug, and the kindness and love that shines in the sisters' eyes, is what keeps people coming back each week."

The sisters credit their parents with instilling generosity in them. "No matter how hungry we were, Daddy taught us that we should always be prepared to help someone needier," they say.

How can you help the poor and the needy with the generosity of your heart and your hands?

Those who are generous are blessed.
(Proverbs 22:9)

Counselor, show me how to aid the poor, including the working poor who can barely make ends meet.

Crossing the Time Line?

Carl Honoré spotted an ad for children's books with one-minute bedtime stories. What a time-saver, he recalls thinking, but then almost immediately felt: "Have I gone insane?"

The personal epiphany prompted Honoré to write *In Praise of Slowness*, a book about our culture's addiction to "more-better-faster" and what some people are doing to inoculate themselves against it.

"The secret is balance, staying calm and unflustered even when circumstances force us to speed up," Honoré explains, stressing the great need to appreciate the "now"–to live present in every moment of a day.

In his own life, this journalist and author has cut down on time in front of the television, has added 10-minute breaks to his work day, and often does "speed checks" to see if the quality of the moment could be improved by slowing down.

How will you spend each moment of this day most wisely?

Know the God of your father, and serve Him with single mind and willing heart; for the Lord searches every mind, and understands every plan and thought. (1 Chronicles 28:9)

Help me to know Your presence, Eternal Lord, from the start to the finish of this day.

Winning Every Day

To win an election, you need more votes than your opponent; a baseball game, more runs than the other team; in life, try tackling these ideas:

- Listen more than you talk.
- Give more than you get.
- Smile more than you frown.
- Compliment more than you criticize.
- Be fascinated more than you're frustrated.
- Be accepting more than rejecting.
- "Walk the walk" more than you "talk the talk."
- See the cup "half full" more than "half empty."
- Think "we" more than "me."
- Help more than you hinder.
- Work more than you whine.
- Laugh more than you cry.
- Believe in yourself more than you doubt.
- Above all, love more than you ever have.

I took them up in My arms...I was to them like those who lift infants to their cheeks. I bent down to them and fed them. (Hosea 11:3,4)

We give thanks for Your love, Father, which is more than we can understand.

A Father's Advice

Jay Ratliff came to appreciate his father's oft-repeated advice while he was a junior high school baseball player: "Know what you're going to do with the ball before you get it."

The value of these words first began to dawn on Ratliff during one particular championship game with the outcome in the balance. At a tense moment he saw his father in the stands pointing to his head.

"What? Is he crazy? Now?" thought the young first baseman. "I'm supposed to stop and think about every possible thing that could happen on the next play–now?" But he did think through his options and when the time came made a great play.

Ratliff's attention to detail and his ability to anticipate problems served him well as he went on to a successful business career. He credits his father's advice with making "all the difference in my life."

As much as you can, plan ahead.

Hear instruction and be wise. (Proverbs 8:33)

Inspire parents to offer good advice and their children to accept it, Abba.

Thanksgiving: Your Family or Mine?

Thanksgiving can mean relaxing times, good food and the company of loved ones, or it can mean controversy and conflict.

This is often true for those couples who can't agree on where to celebrate. When, for example, one spouse's family lives in another state the question can get sticky. There can also be questions about who to invite, who brings what food and many more nagging issues.

Jim Auer writing in *Liguorian*, suggests keeping the main purpose of the day in mind—"taking our place with our loved ones at the Thanksgiving table through our togetherness."

Holidays do present challenges: logistical, emotional and spiritual. Remember, as Auer says "grace, God's gracious favor that has come through each one. Sometimes grace does appear and feel precious—but sometimes abrasive and maddening....But it is through such things that we learn the valuable lessons of compassion, forgiveness, and reconciliation."

The Word became flesh and lived among us. (John 1:16)

Precious, abrasive, maddening, joyous, sorrowful, grace of God most high, saturate my whole being that I may become whom I was born to be.

Oprah, A Woman of Influence

When Oprah Winfrey speaks, people listen. When she advises, they follow. When she acts, they observe. Winfrey is an influential role model.

Now the head of a major media company said to be worth over a billion dollars, she remembers her roots. "I am never not aware of who I am, where I've come from," says Winfrey, who acknowledges her debt to those who struggled before her and who helped her along the way.

"I am a colored girl born in Mississippi in 1954 and all that that means: poverty, isolation, discrimination, lack of information, low self-esteem. The expectation for me was to work in white people's kitchens...My responsibility is not just to myself."

You may not have the same international stage as Oprah Winfrey. But you, too, influence others in large ways or small—and in ways that no one else can.

Influence others for good.

Seek good and not evil. (Amos 5:14)

Show me how to influence others to do good, to be good, to be Yours, Holy Wisdom.

Age, Disease Can't Slow Her Down

After Jeannette Goulet lost her beloved husband, she prayed to God for something to occupy her time and attention. Goulet's prayer was answered and then some.

She has never been busier. She spends up to 12 hours a day sewing quilts for the poor. Goulet, who professes that she's always kept herself busy and is a person who "gets bored on vacations," provides warmth and love to the needy through her soft, colorful quilts.

Despite suffering from cancer and osteoarthritis, she works daily to blend the fabrics and stuffing materials to craft her creations which take hours to sew. "I get more out of this than I give," she says. "It's a beautiful pastime." Her count: over 450 quilts and counting.

How well do you cope with life's challenges? Do you strive to overcome them? Turn them into opportunities?

Be strong and courageous. (Joshua 1:6)

Jesus, keep me focused on the positive in my life.

Presidents Speak about God

From the earliest days of the United States of America, every president has publicly recognized the dependence of this nation on God. Here are a few excerpts from some of their Inaugural Addresses:

George Washington: "In this first official act my fervent supplications to that Almighty Being Who rules over the universe..."

Thomas Jefferson: "Acknowledging and adoring an overruling Providence...May that Infinite Power...lead our councils to what is best."

Abraham Lincoln: "With firmness in the right as God gives us to see the light, let us strive on to finish the work we are in."

Franklin Roosevelt: "We humbly ask the blessing of God...May He guide me in the days to come."

Let us acknowledge our reliance on God through our prayers, our words and our actions.

Cast your burden on the Lord. (Psalm 55:22)

Eternal Lord, thank You for Your unfailing care. Help us share Your mercy with our brothers and sisters of every nation, of every belief.

Part of the Puzzle

Holidays are a time for family traditions–and for some that means taking the time to help others.

Margaret and Larry Timoney started a project to provide Thanksgiving meal deliveries to shut-ins. Working through Catholic Charities' St. John's Breadline in Springfield, Illinois, they have seen to it that as many as 50 elderly people have a turkey dinner with all the fixings each year. Even after Larry Timoney died, Margaret Timoney and their six children–and grandchildren–have kept up the tradition.

Margaret Timoney says, "You're an extension of God's hands. We're grateful that we're capable of going on and helping someone else that day. We're only a little part (but)…Everybody is a little piece in God's puzzle."

We are all part of God's plan and even if it seems like a puzzle to us, we can be sure that He can see the big picture.

I was hungry and you gave Me food, I was thirsty and you gave Me something to drink. (Matthew 25:35)

Merciful Father, show us how to imitate Your loving kindness as we serve our brothers and sisters in need.

The Bittersweet Side of Chocolate

We've come a long way from the days when chocolate meant a simple, milk-chocolate candy bar bought for a few pennies from a corner grocery store.

The U.S. chocolate industry is a multi-billion dollar enterprise. And, with the rise of specialty and gourmet brands, consumers' increasingly discriminating taste has made dark chocolate popular, resulting in a highly competitive business.

In 1803, German chemist and dietary expert Baron Justus von Leibig noted, "Chocolate is the perfect food, and a beneficent restorer of exhausted power...but it must be carefully prepared and its quality must be good." Now we know that dark chocolate is rich in iron, magnesium and zinc as well as flavonoid antioxidants.

Healthy or not, chocolate, like any sweet treat, is best savored in moderation. But, then, moderation is usually a good idea for most aspects of life.

In everything you do be moderate.
(Sirach 31:22)

Help me treat my body with respect, Divine Physician.

The Neediest Need Us

Each year, *The New York Times* sponsors its Neediest Cases Fund for people who need a ray of hope in difficult circumstances.

Donations are distributed to selected non-profit organizations. In turn, those agencies help families such as Ramona Perez'. Though she has a degree from a university in her native Dominican Republic, the divorced mother of a teenaged son and daughter has had to work two low-wage jobs since immigrating to the U.S. in 1994. She came here to get medical care for her daughter who has sickle cell anemia.

"She's been working hard for us for a long time," said her son. Perez' daughter added, "I want to be a mother just like her." The Neediest Cases Fund helped the family with two months' rent.

There are people and causes that need your money and your time. You have neighbors who are in desperate need of mercy–and justice. Stand up for them.

(Cain) said...am I my brother's keeper? (Genesis 4:9)

Remind us, Abba, that we are our brothers' and sisters' keepers; answerable to You, our Father, for each other's well-being.

Mr. Thanksgiving

Robert Vogelbaugh has about 2,000 friends over for Thanksgiving.

The Illinois social worker and grocery store owner started a community Thanksgiving celebration in 1971 when he found that most of his customers, elderly persons who lived alone, would also spend Thanksgiving Day alone. In that first year, Vogelbaugh served turkey and trimmings to 12 customers.

These days the free dinner is set up in the food court of a shopping mall to accommodate the crowds. Vogelbaugh recruits volunteers and raises some $8,000 to pay for the turkeys alone.

He also writes hundreds of thank-you notes to contributors and volunteers alike. And he receives thanks from volunteer families who say the meal taught them and their children "the true meaning of Thanksgiving."

Thanksgiving may be just one day on the calendar, but giving thanks should be a daily action.

(Jesus) took the seven loaves and the fish; and after giving thanks He broke them and gave them to the disciples, and the disciples gave them to the crowds. (Matthew 15:36)

Loving Lord, thanks for all my blessings.

What It Takes To Survive

What does it take to survive tough times? Why do some pull through while others go under?

In his book *Collapse: How Societies Choose to Fail or Succeed,* Jared Diamond writes about how and why certain societies became extinct.

The trees on Easter Island were needed to control soil erosion, to enable agriculture and for building canoes. The canoes were needed for fishing, an important source of sustenance. Once the inhabitants of Easter Island chopped down all the trees they had sealed their fate. They had failed to protect a precious resource.

Diamond writes of other societies who paid dearly for depleting their resources.

We face similar concerns. All natural resources are precious. It's up to each one of us to practice wise stewardship and to encourage our neighbors—and our local, state and federal governments to do their share as well.

The heavens are the Lord's heavens, but the earth He has given to human beings.
(Psalm 115:16)

Inspire us to live frugally, stretching and sharing resources for the long-term benefit of all, Divine Creator.

A Coach Who Cares

When Mario Mendez, a teacher's assistant at Sierra Vista Elementary School in Reno, Nevada, realized that students needed to develop self-esteem and discipline, he decided to do something about it. He began a soccer league.

Mendez supported the program for fourth through sixth graders in the largely Hispanic school by selling candy and ice pops. His wife Rosalba washed uniforms and local police donated equipment.

But before the youngsters were allowed to participate in a practice or game, Mendez checks that their homework is done. One player said, "I was never that good in math, but I like it a little better now since Coach came to our math class to help out."

Interested and caring adults can make a world of difference to children. It means time and effort, but the results may be incalculable.

The Lord your God will...bless the fruit of your womb. (Deuteronomy 7:12,13)

Abba, encourage us to use our talents and opportunities to nurture Your children.

A String of Thanksgiving

When problems get the best of you, the best solution can be a dose of gratitude.

That's what Kathy Eblen realized as she sat in church the Sunday before Thanksgiving, worrying about family finances. Writing in *Guideposts,* she says she prayed, "I'm fixated on my problems, Lord. Help me to be thankful."

That's when she thought of the answer: popcorn! At Thanksgiving, Eblen put a dish of unpopped kernels at each place. The centerpiece for the table was an empty bowl.

Each member of the family took turns mentioning things for which they were grateful. With each contribution ("Our dog, Cody."... "Bedtime stories Dad reads us."...) a kernel was put in the bowl. After the family bought their Christmas tree they popped the corn and together strung a garland of "blessing popcorn" that they hung on their tree.

The simplest gesture of thanksgiving can change our attitude. Express your gratitude often.

Be thankful...And whatever you do...do everything in the name of the Lord Jesus, giving thanks to God the Father. (Colossians 3:15,17)

O generous and gracious God, thank You for Your unending love, Your unceasing mercy.

Yet Another Benefit of Prayer

Did you know prayer can help keep a marriage secure and happy? In a letter on marriage, Catholic Bishop John Kinney of St. Cloud, Minnesota, says that couples have told him "Prayer is the glue that held us together."

Here are some guidelines for putting the power of prayer into your marriage:

- Seeking common ground in prayer is vital, especially in an inter-denominational or inter-faith marriage. Consider starting with the Our Father. The prayer should work for both of you.
- Take it slowly, beginning with prayer at dinner time. Take turns praying for your needs as individuals and as a couple; for children, relatives, family friends and neighbors.
- Allow for silence. Allow God to speak in that sacred silence.
- End with a hug and a kiss.

Our relationship with God and with people is intertwined. Let's make an effort to pray with and for one another often.

God is love, and those who abide in love abide in God, and God abides in them. (1 John 4:16)

Eternal Father, help all couples pray with one another and to grow with one another.

Comfort for the Children of War

Wars bring widespread pain, suffering and destruction. Children are wars' most innocent victims. Fortunately, there are also compassionate and generous people who look for ways to comfort them.

Episcopal Life reports on the efforts of doll maker Mary Pope Jones who has "offered her pattern so others could help make comfort toys for kids in war zones."

Jones runs a growing operation from her Wapiti, Wyoming, home and has shipped dolls to Iraq, Haiti, Sudan, Bethlehem and Gaza, among other places.

Dolls and other comforting toys are wonderful. But the ideal would be a world with no war; no children damaged by war. Until the day of universal peace is achieved, start or support projects that comfort the world's war-damaged children.

They shall beat their swords into plowshares, and their spears into pruning hooks; nation shall not lift up sword against nation, neither shall they learn war any more. (Micah 4:3)

God of peace, help the nations understand the futility of violence and war and the value of peace and cooperation.

Making Thanksgiving Real

The spiritual side of Thanksgiving is often lost in the fun and work of the feast for family and friends.

In *Today's Christian Woman* magazine, Kate Bryant told how her family gained a new perspective: "One Thanksgiving I asked everyone to write down something God had done for them the previous year. We read these aloud and then recited a phrase from Psalm 136: 'Give thanks to the Lord, for He is good. His love endures forever.'

"It sounded something like this: 'He helped me pass my math class. Give thanks to the Lord, for He is good. His loves endures forever'. 'Even though I got laid off and I'm still looking for a job, God's provided everything I need. Give thanks to the Lord, for He is good. His love endures forever.

"Giving thanks became real for us that year," Bryant concluded.

Go beyond words. Give thanks from your heart.

O give thanks to the Lord, for He is good, for His steadfast love endures forever. ...It is He who remembered us...and rescued us. (Psalm 136:1,23,24)

Mighty and merciful God, thank You for Your many gifts, especially the gift of Yourself.

Abraham Lincoln and the Pilgrims

In school, we learned that the Pilgrims and the Native Americans ate the first Thanksgiving feast together.

But the tradition of sitting down with family and friends in front of enormous amounts of food each November didn't become an official American tradition until much later.

In an October 3, 1863 proclamation, President Abraham Lincoln declared the fourth Thursday of November a "Day of Thanksgiving" for all Americans "to thank God for His bountiful blessings to our nation." The United States was engaged in its Civil War, so Lincoln's proclamation also sought the "Almighty Hand to heal the wounds of the nation and to restore it...to the full enjoyment of peace, harmony, tranquility."

Thanksgiving is a wonderful holiday, but every day is the right time to offer thanks for the blessings in our lives—and to ask for peace in our hearts, our homes, our nation and our world.

Be thankful....With gratitude in your hearts. ...Do everything in the name of the Lord Jesus, giving thanks to God the Father through Him. (Colossians 3:15,16,17)

All thanks and all praise are Yours, Abba.

Benefits of the Other Job

Alan Guarino of Marlboro, New York, is the chief executive officer of an executive recruiting firm. The rewards are fine, but it's his other job that gives him the most satisfaction.

Nine days a year, he puts on a t-shirt and tool belt and, often with his wife and children, repairs poor families' homes in Kentucky as part of the Capuchin Youth and Family Ministries Center. Once a month, he also volunteers overnight at a local homeless shelter.

He schedules those volunteer days and nights just as he would business or family commitments. Guarino says, "Rather than just giving money to charity, (any one) can make it part of their life." He adds, "It's just tremendously rewarding... giving to those in need."

How can you make generosity with your time and talents a part of your everyday life?

Where your treasure is, there your heart will be also. (Matthew 6:21)

Show us how to find the time for generous service as well as family and self, Holy Spirit.

About the "Mall-ing" of America

Drive through most American towns and a disturbing realization dawns: they've begun to resemble each other and have lost their uniqueness; malls and chain stores have proliferated.

One day, Bob Lang pulled into the parking lot of his printing and publishing business in an office park off a highway. Looking at the cookie-cutter strip malls and generic, impersonal landscape, he thought, "How can my employees be creative when there is nothing around them to inspire them?"

He bought an old building near Main Street in Delafield, Wisconsin. In time, other small-business owners joined him. They helped revitalize the town, recapturing much of its original sense of community as well as its commerce.

"Mom and Pop" stores and businesses and the people who own them contribute greatly toward making a town into a community. Support your neighbors in as many ways as you can.

Joseph also went from the town of Nazareth in Galilee to Judea, to the city of David called Bethlehem...with Mary. (Luke 2:4,5)

Jesus, carpenter of the town of Nazareth, help us to conserve and to rebuild our cities and towns.

Fasting: Why Do it?

Followers of nearly every religion observe fasting at one time or another, or, at least, recognize its merits. Yet most people may not know the rationale behind the practice.

For many, fasting represents a way to get closer to God. Says Rev. John Dietzen, "Food and drink are blessings God obviously wants us to enjoy. ...Fasting, therefore, is a way of telling God we're really serious about what we pray for."

For others, fasting is a way to experience the deprivation others at home and abroad experience daily, to deepen compassion for them and to build up the determination to help them.

When you fast ponder the 58th chapter of the Book of Isaiah. Remember, your spirit needs nourishment, attention and care as much as the body.

If you remove the yoke from among you, the pointing of the finger, the speaking of evil, if you offer your food to the hungry and satisfy the needs of the afflicted, then...the Lord will guide you continually, and satisfy your needs. (Isaiah 58:9-10,11)

Spirit of Hope, strengthen our choice to fast from injustice.

Stop the World I'm on a Subway Car

The weekend had been non-stop activity for Monica Glick—again. The week ahead promised more of the same. All she wanted was just to stop and relax—even if just for five minutes.

Suddenly, on her New York City subway train this Monday morning, there was a man walking through and selling toothpaste. He was followed by a woman peddling batteries and $1 candy bars. Glick smiled that her train had transformed into a mobile shopping mall.

Next, there was beautiful music—a young man on the train was playing the clarinet. Glick's "to do" list faded, and her stress drifted away.

As she and the clarinet player exited the train together at the next stop, Glick checked her watch—she had gotten her five minutes.

No matter how busy we are, it's important to spend a few minutes enjoying the simple pleasures every day brings.

A ruby seal in a setting of gold is a concert of music...a seal of emerald in a rich setting of gold is the melody of music with good wine. (Sirach 32:5,6)

Rushing winds, calm breezes, instrumental music and song remind me of Your presence, Lord of Life. Thank You.

One Day at a Time

Dave and Linda Giere, were preparing dinner for friends and family. As the guests began to arrive, Dave discovered Linda in the kitchen, staring into space, most of the meal unprepared.

Because his wife was usually so conscientious and punctual, Dave Giere was alarmed. Something wasn't right.

"Something" turned out to be Alzheimer's disease. Devastated, they planned for the care Linda Giere, who had long periods of disorientation and confusion, would increasingly need.

On her more lucid days, she starts each day with a prayer: "Lord, you know I'm here and you know I love my family and my life." At night, she prays, "This was a good day. Thank You."

There are always opportunities for complaints and pessimism. Yet, in the most unlikely circumstances, each moment can be a cause for celebration and thanks.

Remember your Creator in the days of your youth, before the days of trouble come, and the years draw near when you will say, "I have no pleasure in them." (Ecclesiastes 12:1)

Guide all who care for those with Alzheimer and other dementias, Holy Spirit.

To Save Lives...

18-year-old Mallory Jones, a Mississippi high school senior, was devastated when her friend Chase was killed driving home drunk from a bar in July 2003. That same year, one-third of teen drivers who died were killed in alcohol-related accidents.

Instead of allowing the tragedy to get the better of her Mallory decided to create *Businesses to Save Youth*—or BUSY for short. It's a service in which students act as designated drivers for teens that have been drinking.

Mallory recognized that many of these accidents happen because most kids don't want to call their parents to pick them up. Based on 10 strict guidelines, this confidential student-only service is community-backed and partially funded by local businesses.

Seek to create opportunities from life's adversities, especially when there's the chance to save lives.

Jesus said to them, "Fill the jars with water." ...Now draw some out, and take it to the chief steward." (John 2:7,8)

Jesus, who drank wine and changed water into it, help parents teach their children to be temperate through their own example.

Extreme Cuisine

The wild abalone is not found on fine-dining menus, and most people would be hard pressed to describe what it is or how it tastes. In fact, it cannot be sold legally and is unobtainable in restaurants or fish markets.

Though scallop-sized farmed abalone is available commercially, the wild variety is said to have a more delicate flavor. Perhaps its elusive qualities are what drive some devotees of this rare delicacy to plunge into the frigid, turbulent waters of the Northern California coast; to walk treacherous ledges, digging under craggy rocks to capture even one wild abalone.

Sadly, the abalone's appeal may be one cause for its demise: its future is threatened due to poachers and over-fishing.

It's important to consider the greater good; to ask yourself: Is this something I really need? Will my consumption help or hurt the environment? Thinking beyond the self can influence others to do likewise.

One does not live by bread alone, but by every word that comes from the mouth of the Lord. (Deuteronomy 8:3)

Help us to celebrate, not ravage, Your gifts to us in Nature, Creator.

Lunchtime for Body and Soul

Next time you break for lunch, try to allow time not only for the sustenance of daily bread but also for time to nourish your spirit with a bit of daily renewal. You probably have ideas of your own, but consider these suggestions from *Body & Soul* magazine:

- Don't wait until you're starving to take a break. Choose light, healthy fare.

- Take a short walk to lift your mood, boost your spirits, and maybe work off a few calories. Three 10-minute bursts of exercise throughout the day are beneficial.

- S t r e t c h. Massage your temples, forehead, and scalp. Breathe deeply.

- Meditate briefly, in a park if possible.

Relaxed and restored you can better face the rest of the day.

It is fitting to eat and drink and find enjoyment in all the toil with which one toils. (Ecclesiastes 5:18)

Redeemer, remind us to balance work and leisure during the work day.

The Courage to Respond to Her True Calling

Jeri Oliver, a pharmaceutical rep, was selling HIV/AIDS drugs to physicians, when she met a leader of the Ugandan community in the Minneapolis-St. Paul area. Through him she learned of the plight of Africa's millions of AIDS orphans. "The number of children affected made my blood run cold," she says. "I am a mother...I knew I had to do something."

She completed a 75-mile walk through South Africa to raise money for AIDS research; began an arts project with Ugandan AIDS and war orphans; took in four teenaged African boys; and started the non-profit Illume International to raise money for the education of Africa's orphans.

Although her work is sometimes discouraging, Oliver perseveres. She says, "we have to take it on faith that we can make a difference, and that one person's actions can inspire others."

Where and how can you make a difference?

"Who sinned, this man or his parents, that he was born blind?" Jesus answered, "Neither...he was born blind so that God's works might be revealed in him. (John 9:2-3)

Lord God, inspire many to work for both the cure and prevention of HIV/AIDS.

Coming to Christmas

Since Advent means "coming," as we think about Jesus' coming at Christmas, let's consider the words of the late Pope John Paul II: "Advent...helps us to understand fully the value and meaning of the mystery of Christmas. It is not just about commemorating the historical event, which occurred some 2,000 years ago in a little village of Judea. Instead, it is necessary to understand that the whole of our life must be an 'advent,' a vigilant awaiting of the final coming of Christ.

"To predispose our mind to welcome the Lord who, as we say in the Creed, one day will come to judge the living and the dead, we must learn to recognize Him as present in the events of daily life. Therefore, Advent is, so to speak, an intense training that directs us decisively toward Him who already came, who will come, and who comes continuously."

Welcome the Lord at every moment, in every person.

Our Lord, come! (1 Corinthians 16:22)

Jesus, Savior, you are welcome in my heart and in my whole being. Live in me always!

A Box for Jared

Jared McMullen was only 5 years old when he was diagnosed with incurable brain cancer.

One day a neighbor and her children, wanting to show their concern, filled a shoebox with small toys and art supplies and brought it to him at the hospital. Jared asked, "How come other kids here don't have toys to play with?"

After Jared's death in 2000, classmates at Our Lady of Victory School in State College, Pennsylvania, joined his parents in creating the Jared Box Project. Now students from dozens of schools fill plastic boxes with puzzles, coloring books, games and other fun items for boys and girls undergoing chemotherapy or dialysis and bring them to hospitals. By the end of 2005, over 10,000 boxes had reached children in 21 states.

Grief exacts a terrible toll. But grief can also motivate us to help others who need what we have to give.

He took her by the hand and said to her, "Talitha cum"...And immediately the girl got up. (Mark 5:41)

Do not let my heart's grief overwhelm me, Spirit of Comfort. Instead, show me how to help others heal.

When Moving the Mountain Isn't an Option

For three months out of the year, all sunlight to the town of Rattenberg, Austria, is blocked out by a nearby mountain. Depression rates soar, and the town's younger residents have been moving away.

A local company, however, has engineered a solution; a system of 30 rotating mirrors is being installed in Rattenberg and neighboring towns. The mirrors will reflect sunlight into "hot spots" in Rattenberg, where residents can soak up sunlight during the town's "dark" months. Villagers will even be able to watch the sun set in reflection on the sides of certain buildings.

Some problems are truly too mountainous to deal with head-on. Yet, in most cases, there's a solution. All it takes is a little ingenuity and determination.

If you have faith the size of a mustard seed, you will say to this mountain, 'Move from here to here', and it will move; and nothing will be impossible for you. (Matthew 17:20)

Lord, help me to find my way around those impediments that challenge me.

Being Yourself

It takes courage to be yourself. Here's a story about one man who knew that.

A pious old man, Rabbi Susya, became fearful as death drew near. Friends chided him, "What! Are you afraid that you'll be reproached that you weren't Moses?"

"No," the rabbi replied, "that I was not Susya."

While it's true that too often people use the sentiment that "I've got to be me" as an excuse for selfish behavior, we really do need to be true to ourselves. Nobody is born into this world with exactly your abilities or opportunities: you are an unrepeatable gift of God.

Choose to live your life as fully and as well as you can, not only for your own sake, but also for the good of others. Never be afraid to be yourself—the unique person that our Creator means you to be.

Honesty comes home to those who practice it. (Sirach 27:9)

Watch over me, Spirit of Wisdom. Guide my desires and my decisions so that my life fulfills Your plans for me.

Dear Santa

The U. S. postal service has delivered more than 120,000 letters to Alaska's Gabby Gaborik. Believe it or not, he expects twice that amount by year's end.

Gaborik is not famous; in fact, most of the people whose letters are sitting in his garage awaiting an answer don't even know his real name.

That's because Gaborik heads his local Lions Club's "Santa's Mailbag" project. Ever since North Pole, Alaska, got its own post office, letters addressed to "Santa" have been pouring in. Gaborik answers a large portion of them.

Often, he'll respond to particularly touching requests from needy or troubled children by contacting Lions Clubs near the writer's home. They in turn will fulfill the requests if possible.

Encourage young children to hope by reaching out to them with your help.

**A generous person will be enriched.
(Proverbs 11:25)**

How can we be "Santa Claus" to those who otherwise would lack one, Infant Savior?

How to Get Organized

Sense the need for greater organization in your life? Another "to-do" list may not be the only solution. According to Kathy Peel, author of *The Family Manager Takes Charge,* a "Not-to-Do" list may be as helpful.

For example, Peel says that by listing non-essential tasks, you can free up time for essential ones. She also suggests:

Work with, not against, your daily rhythms and schedule. If you're a morning person, do your most important work then.

Practice the power of 10. If there are no long stretches of time in the foreseeable future, snatch 10 minutes here and there to progress toward completing a big project.

Do it now. Whenever possible, especially concerning unpleasant tasks, make this your motto.

Organizing your life means honoring time, the stuff of which life's made. How can you make your day calmer and more productive?

I have calmed and quieted my soul.
(Psalm 131:2)

Generous God, help me treat the life You've given me as the precious gift it is.

Up From Slavery

Harriet Ross Tubman survived the brutal childhood of a slave in Dorchester County, Maryland, in the 1820s: overwork, severe punishment, little schooling. In 1848, she escaped.

Over the next decade as a conductor on the Underground Railroad, she made about 20 trips and rescued more than 300 slaves. A $40,000 reward was posted for her capture.

In the 1860s she appeared at anti-slavery meetings and women's rights meetings before fleeing to Canada. But she returned, serving the Union as nurse, soldier and spy.

Despite her labors and sacrifices on behalf of the Union, Tubman did not receive a government pension until 30 years after the Civil War had ended. She used her $20 monthly pension to begin a home, later renamed the Harriet Tubman Home, for the aged and needy.

Are you willing to make sacrifices for the common good?

(Judith) prayed the Lord God of Israel to direct her way for the triumph of His people. (Judith 12:8)

Bless us with many courageous and wise women, Holy Wisdom.

"Abwûn d'bwaschmâja"...

Jesus taught His disciples to pray, saying "Abwûn d'bwaschmâja" ("Our Father in heaven"). Jesus' daily language was Aramaic; the Gospels were written in Greek, translated into Latin and, from the 16th century Reformation on, into English and other languages. Here, with transliterations, is part of the Aramaic Our Father:

Abwûn d'bwaschmâja—O cosmic Birther of all radiance and vibration who fills all realms of sound, light and vibration...

Nethkâdasch schmach—May Your light be experienced in me...

Têtê malkuthach—Your Heavenly Domain approaches...

Nehwê tzevjânach aikâna d'bwaschmâja af b'arha—Let Your will come true—in the universe... just as on earth....

Touch Christianity's Middle Eastern linguistic and spiritual roots. Find a recording of the Aramaic Our Father, and listen to this universal prayer in Jesus' language.

Pray with Jesus—pray with all your heart.

Your Father who is in secret and...sees in secret... knows what you need. (Matthew 6:6,8)

Abba, may Your name be blessed by me, this moment, now.

Making the Worst of Times Better

Jackson, like most little boys, loves fire trucks. So when the World Trade Center was destroyed on September 11, 2001, he drew a picture of one to show the firefighters of Ladder Company 163/Engine 325 how love can overcome grief and sadness.

In the wake of the terrorist attacks, Jackson, who is a high-functioning autistic, saw a flattened fire truck in the rubble of the towers. Jackson sent Company 163 a letter that included a picture of a fire truck, as a way of helping "replace" one of the Company's lost engines.

Grief-stricken Firefighter Kenny Warns happened to read the letter and was so moved, he wrote back. That began a poignant correspondence between a New York City firefighter and a little boy from Akron, Ohio.

Support and love come from the most unexpected places and people.

I will give you my support. (2 Samuel 3:12)

The incidence of autism is increasing, Lord of Life. Inspire researchers to find the causes and the cure.

The Ultimate Sacrifice

Humanitarian relief worker Margaret Hassan was posthumously awarded Ireland's prestigious Tipperary Peace Prize after her abduction and murder in Baghdad, Iraq, in 2004.

"She showed extraordinary courage, tenacity and commitment in her concern for those who were living in the most difficult of circumstances," noted the prize organization.

The Dublin-born Hassan was married to an Iraqi and held Irish, British and Iraqi citizenship. She had lived and worked in Iraq for 30 years, the last 12 as that country's director of operations for Care International.

"The poor people of Iraq will always remember Margaret," said Cardinal Cormac Murphy-O'Connor at a memorial Mass in Westminster Cathedral attended by 2,000 people. "She has become a symbol of goodness in a world crying out for goodness."

Rather than becoming discouraged by war and violence, we need to work–and live–for peace.

The effect of righteousness will be peace. (Isaiah 32:17)

Master, give us the courage to work for peace by being people of justice in our families, our workplaces and our neighborhoods.

Fine Dining in a School Cafeteria?

Hard as it may be to believe, delicious, healthful foods may be coming to a school cafeteria near you.

Thanks to the success of chef Jorge Collazo, who has made lunchtime healthy for nearly 4,000 New York City high school students, more schools are weighing their options to provide more healthful fare in the lunchroom.

At Long Island City High School, Collazo has introduced a salad bar, replaced white bread with whole grain varieties, and has lowered the fat, sugar and salt in virtually all of the school's lunch recipes. Schools across the country are taking notice.

Collazo's philosophy? Simple: the students are his customers and deserve to be treated as such.

Treat young people with respect, and they will do likewise.

Pay to all what is due them...respect to whom respect is due, honor to whom honor is due. (Romans 13:7)

Remind adults to respect young people and to encourage them to respect themselves, Creator of all generations.

Blessed—and Knowing It

Count your blessings. We've all heard those words, but Afton Rorvik of Wheaton, Illinois, found new meaning in them after an encounter with the clerk at the local pharmacy.

Writing in *Guideposts*, Rorvik says that it had been a bad day topped off with a splitting headache. At the cash register, the clerk cheerfully asked, "How are you?" Rather than complain, Rorvik merely replied, "I'm fine. How are you?"

The smiling clerk answered, "I'm richly blessed."

"I thought about the clerk's words all the way home," wrote Rorvik who started thinking about personal blessings. "By evening, I'd come up with dozens. Despite my worries, I knew I was richly blessed, too."

We take so much for granted, but the truth is that God gives us gifts each day of our lives. Even in our darkest hours, God is always there for us. Appreciate His generosity and abiding presence.

He will cover you with His pinions, and under His wings you will find refuge; His faithfulness is a shield. (Psalm 91:4)

Benevolent Father, help me appreciate Your bountiful blessings and protection.

What the World Needs Now...

Diseases like malaria, cholera and typhoid seem distant to most Americans, not much more than headline news.

Not so in Tanzania where 15% of all children under age five die from sudden infections and there is only one doctor for every 40,000 people. While the U. S. lifespan is in the high 70s for both men and women, in Tanzania it is just 41 years.

Maryknoll priest and physician Rev. Peter LeJacq has begun an effort to provide a self-sustaining health care structure in Tanzania. He's planning to build a medical school at the Bugando Referral Hospital, the only hospital for 12 million people in northern Tanzania. Weill Medical College of Cornell University, Rev. LeJacq's alma mater acts as the partner school and the TOUCH foundation, which he began, handles fundraising.

One person can make a difference; love for our fellow human beings is the root of all positive change.

Love one another deeply from the heart. (1 Peter 1:22)

May we live the love You taught us, Christ Jesus, in our daily interaction with others.

Are We There Yet?

Here's a modern fable about a fisherman who lives in a tiny, tropical village and a tourist from far away.

The tourist asked the fisherman how long it took him to catch his basket of fish. "Not very long," replied the fisherman. "Then why don't you stay out longer, and catch fish all day?" asked the tourist, a wealthy businessman. "You could catch enough fish to own your own fleet of boats, and you'd make millions! Then, after a lifetime of success, you'd have accrued enough wealth to retire in a small village, a lot like this one, where you could rest, relax and spend time with your family."

The fisherman paused. "That's interesting," he said. "That's exactly what I do with my spare time, after I've fished enough to feed my family."

How do you define success: exhaustive acquisition? Or time for family and friends and enough food, shelter and clothing?

Give me neither poverty nor riches; feed me with the food that I need, or I shall be full, and deny You...or...poor, and steal, and profane the name of my God. (Proverbs 30:8-9)

Teach me to avoid excess, Holy Wisdom.

It's a Wonderful Life

In *It's A Wonderful Life,* actor Jimmy Stewart played a despairing man, George Bailey, who learned the power of friendship and why we shouldn't give up.

This 1940s Frank Capra film became a heartwarming favorite, in part because it reveals how one person makes a difference in the lives of others without being aware of it.

Stewart later described the impact making the film had on him. In one scene the despondent Bailey cries out "God...I'm not a praying man, but if you're up there and you can hear me, show me the way."

When he said those lines, Stewart felt "the hopelessness of people who had no where to turn" as well as "the power of that prayer, the realization that our Father in heaven is there to help the hopeless."

We're here to befriend and help one another so that all may know it's a wonderful life.

I will help you says the Lord. (Isaiah 41:14)

Help us to be Your instruments in restoring hope to the hopeless, Comforter and Counselor.

More Than One Way to Social Change

Carmen Velasquez was no stranger to adversity. When the Chicagoan visited Fort Madison, Iowa, her mother's hometown, she realized that the "place" of Mexicans was expected to be at the back of the church.

But by the time she was 20, she saw clearly the injustice of it all. Instead of letting her anger fester, she used it to fuel positive action. One of her God-given talents is organizing. So, she became a social activist, and over the next 18 years raised millions of dollars for the Alivio Medical Clinics that help Hispanics who lacked affordable health care.

Velasquez's philosophy on life is simple. "If I can't get through the door, I'll have to use the window."

The effects of racism and prejudice are both cruel and devastating. What constructive action can you take?

Why do you pass judgment on your brother or sister? Or...despise your brother or sister? For we will all stand before the judgment seat of God. (Romans 14:10)

Just and Merciful God, enable me to use my anger at injustice as a spur to work for change.

It BODES Well for Kids

Writer Sheila Murray developed a way to foster responsibility and independence in kids. She uses the word BODES, as in "it bodes well," for parents and their kids in their journey toward responsible adulthood.

B*attles:* Pick your battles; make a big deal only about the big stuff, and let them work through the small stuff on their own.

O*ptions:* Provide youngsters with ample opportunities to make their own decisions.

D*iscipline:* Don't shield your child from punishment; seek guidance however on what's appropriate, if you're unsure.

E*xample:* Kids of all ages learn by example. If you want your child to follow rules, do so yourself.

S*ave:* Help your children to plan, budget and save for expenditures. Teach them that money is a reward for physical or mental labor.

And always, teach with love and creativity.

Teach shrewdness. (Proverbs 1:4)

Help parents have a sense of humor even in the most trying of times, Holy Spirit.

Volunteering: Why Bother?

Why volunteer your time when you can just write a check?

College graduate Matthew Bricker found out through experience that volunteering one's time and talent is a far cry from simply donating money.

While many charities truly need financial support, giving your time to help others, says Bricker, can be a life-changing experience for the volunteer. He built houses for Habitat for Humanity and made soup for a county food-distribution center.

Volunteering is personally fulfilling and enriching, particularly when it correlates with a personal interest or skill.

Finally, Bricker says that the emotional impact of volunteering can be profound. He says, "Giving of yourself to others through volunteering enables your spirit to grow and deepen in a way that makes true service infinitely valuable."

What a wonderful summary of the benefits of volunteering!

Bear one another's burdens. (Galatians 6:2)

Inspire youth to give their time and talents volunteering, Jesus of Nazareth.

Crafting History in Glass

Michael Davis is a glass artist who specializes in creating replicas of antique glass, sometimes from mere shards of the original. Davis' craft involves not only technique and care, but research into the history of each unique piece he aims to recreate.

What makes Davis even more unusual among fellow artisans is that while most glass experts focus on a single technique, such as blowing or bending glass, Davis has developed mastery of several production methods. The diversity and depth of his talent and competence has made him a sought-after artist not only among historians and preservationists, but also by homeowners seeking to add unique beauty to their homes.

You, too, have special qualities and abilities. Think about them and how you can develop them to bring out the best in yourself.

Listen to Me...who have been borne by Me from your birth, carried from the womb...I have made, and I will bear; I will carry and will save. (Isaiah 46:3,4)

Help me remember that there is only one person like me in the universe, Creator and Lover.

Use Your Helping Hands

Everyone needs a helping hand sometime.

Kevin Isakson was working in a pet store where he became friendly with an elderly, wheelchair-using customer. The man asked the Utah State University student if he would shovel the snow off his walk. Isakson agreed and did it all winter without taking any money.

Thinking about other people in the area who needed similar help, he put an ad in the paper for volunteers and for those who needed Helping Hands–the name of his project. There was a good response, including a donation of snow shovels from a local hardware store.

Isakson was delighted. "I just tried to start something up, and it worked," he said.

The desire to do good and a degree of enthusiasm may be all that's necessary to get the ball rolling. What good can you do today?

Come, you that are blessed by my Father, inherit the kingdom...for I was hungry and you gave Me food, I was thirsty and you gave me...drink...I was sick and you took care of Me. (Matthew 25:34,35,36)

Loving Father, remind me that I have a responsibility to care about and for my brothers and sisters.

What Does Your Company Say About You?

Take a close look at those with whom you associate. Do they share your values? Are they edifying? Does it matter? According to Orlane Benau, it matters a great deal.

Benau, realized that teens in her Harlem, New York, neighborhood were faced with hard choices and enormous pressure in deciding to avoid drug addiction or promiscuity. A lack of positive role models and alternatives exacerbated the situation.

But, Benau says, "If people around you are doing positive things, eventually you'll want to be positive, too." With this in mind, Benau founded a dance group for teenage girls called Mahogany, after the durable, beautiful, reddish-brown wood. The group gave neighborhood teenaged girls a viable, productive and fun way to stay out of trouble while building self esteem and dancing.

Benau shares her time and talent to help create positive results in others' lives.

How can you help youngsters find a better future?

Bad company ruins good morals.
(1 Corinthians 15:33)

Allow me to see hope rather than despair, solutions rather than problems, and love rather than hate, Divine Master.

Going Beyond Grief

Holidays are difficult times for people grieving the loss of a loved one. But there are ways to experience healing.

One woman whose adult daughter had died suddenly started a new Christmas tradition for her family. She gave each person money to be used to help a needy person in a creative way. When they gathered for the holiday dinner, each person had a life-giving story to tell. The ritual became a way to remember and to create new memories.

The late Rev. Henri Nouwen wrote, "We will suffer, and suffer with one another, but in doing so we will uncover...the presence of a God whose consolation keeps us going. ...Pain suffered alone feels very different from pain suffered alongside another. Even when the pain stays, we know how great the difference is if another draws close, if another shares with us in it."

Share your grief. Share your joy.

Come to Me, all you that are...carrying heavy burdens...Take My yoke upon you...for My yoke is easy, and My burden is light. (Matthew 11:28,29,30)

Show me how to reach out to those in emotional and physical pain, Spirit of Comfort.

Seeing a Grand Oasis

On Christmas Eve, 1969, as Apollo 8 circled the moon, on-board cameras televised the mother planet, 231,000 miles away. Capt. James Lovell remarked that the earth looked like a "grand oasis in the big vastness of space."

Near the end of the broadcast, Col. Frank Borman said that the crew had a special message for "all the people back on earth."

Then Maj. William Anders started reading from the book of Genesis, "In the beginning, God created the heavens and the earth..." The three space travelers took turns reading the Biblical creation narrative, ending with, "and God saw that it was good."

"Good night, good luck, Merry Christmas!" concluded Col. Borman. "God bless all of you–all of you on the good earth."

This truly is God's good earth–and ours. God has given us the responsibility of caring for our planet. Let us serve our Creator well.

> **God called the dry land Earth, and the waters...Seas. And God saw that it was good. (Genesis 1:10)**

> *Creator of all, thank You for Your magnificent gift to us, our beloved earth. Do not let us fail You in caring for our home's welfare and its future.*

Music at Christmas

Does music change your mood? Lift your spirits? Have you ever recalled another time on hearing a familiar tune?

For one mother of seven children, the songs she associates with Christmas and hears year after year transport her back in time. Or, as she puts it, "they renew the child in me." *O Holy Night. Silver Bells. Silent Night. Go Tell It on the Mountain. Hark! The Herald Angels Sing.* Those are some of the songs that move her.

What moves you? Music has the power to touch our deepest being and tap into our emotions. The happy thoughts of childhood holidays and summers; memories of a first love; poignant reminders of loss; times filled with joyful reminiscence or spiritual comfort.

This Christmas, enjoy the beauty of music and let it fill your heart and soul with gladness as you contemplate the birth of the Son of God.

And suddenly there was with the angel a multitude of the heavenly host praising God and saying, 'Glory to God in the highest heaven, and on earth peace among those whom He favors.' (Luke 2:13-14)

Thank you, God, for Your gifts at Christmas and every day—above all, for the gift of Yourself.

A Heart for Giving

Hundreds of thousands of people in southeast Asia died when a tsunami struck just after Christmas in 2004. Millions were left homeless.

Not only governments, but individuals responded with open hearts and hands. Many children came up with their own ways to help.

To let the youngsters in the ravaged areas know that they were not forgotten, students at Linwood Middle School in North Brunswick, New Jersey, drew pictures and created collages and Valentines to send them.

Meanwhile, students from St. Nicholas School in Altos Hills, California, came up with a "Helping Hearts" project. They made and sold beautiful Valentine cards to raise money for tsunami relief efforts.

Every one of us has the responsibility to help those in need, no matter our age or the circumstances of our lives. People are counting on us. Let's do the best we can as often as we can.

Your prayers and your alms have ascended as a memorial before God. (Acts 10:4)

Jesus, show me how to imitate Your loving kindness. Show me how to love my neighbor as myself today.

Quiet, Please!

When Elizabeth Ficocelli, mother of four sons, says she needs a break from the demands of motherhood, she's not kidding.

But Ficocelli's idea of "getting away from it all" is more than taking a walk or going out with friends. Each year, this innovative mom packs her bags and heads off for four days of peaceful prayer and contemplation at a rural Kentucky monastery.

Interestingly, Ficocelli didn't realize just how much she needed the peace and quiet until she was at the monastery. She says, "By the third day, I was finally acclimated to the routine of monastic life," as well as the quiet surroundings. The profound experience enabled her to "bring some of that same peacefulness back to (her) life as a wife and mother."

Everyone needs to recharge their spiritual batteries. Try solitude when things are overwhelming. Solutions and answers may come from the silence.

It is good that one should wait quietly for the salvation of the Lord. (Lamentations 3:26)

Calm my soul, Prince of Peace, just as You calmed the rough waters of Gennesaret.

Reach Out to the Community

Dr. Gloria WilderBrathwaite, the medical director of the Washington D.C. Children's Health Project, became a physician because "I wanted to help somebody, you know, just one person."

A gifted if impoverished student, WilderBrathwaite was the first from her family to attend college. She went to Howard University as a microbiology-chemistry major; masters degrees in genetics and in public health followed. Then there was Georgetown medical school.

Dr. WilderBrathwaite has spent the last 15 years bringing a mobile pediatric clinic to Washington, D.C.'s impoverished Anacostia neighborhood.

Think of creative ways to bring about positive social change. Help just one person, yourself, to change, then, help others change their lives for the better.

Honor physicians for their services, for the Lord created them; for their gift of healing comes from the Most High. (Sirach 38:1-2)

Help me create positive change in myself, Author of Life and Liberty. Then help me reach out to help others.

United in Words

New York's Queensborough Public Library has an English literacy program to help immigrant mothers support their children's literacy as they themselves become fluent in English.

While the mothers differ in their country of origin, first language, culture and customs, they share a common desire to learn to read, speak and write English and to support their children as they learn English.

Although the classes begin with difficult moments, by the end of the year, the students are blooming. According to the program director, Silvana Vasconcelos, "Parents learn best when they learn with their children."

Focus on what unites us to other Americans, including our language. Celebrate differences, too. The United States is a nation of immigrants, beginning with those who walked across the land bridge from Asia to North America many centuries ago.

Have unity of spirit, sympathy, love...a tender heart, and a humble mind. ...Turn away from evil and do good. ...Seek peace and pursue it. (1 Peter 3:8,11)

May we Americans celebrate what unites us even as we recognize and celebrate our individuality, Holy God.

Clean Your Room...Please!

If you are a parent, it's a good bet you've been face to face with procrastination. It seems as though no one puts off doing tasks the way kids can. But rather than becoming frustrated, consider the following:

- Explain enough—what the job is; when it's to be completed; and the consequences if not done.
- Be sure tasks and chores are age-appropriate.
- Have clear rules and expectations, especially for homework.
- Give responsibility.
- Set up rewards and punishments
- Have a jobs list.
- Be flexible. If there is too much to do, children will feel the pressure even more than you do. If your child looks tired, or is struggling with a homework assignment, move the task to the next day lovingly, without resentment.

Train children in the right way. (Proverbs 22:6)

Protect the little ones among us, Jesus, Child of Nazareth.

Obligations to World's People

The real issues facing the world are "daily bread, shelter, water, work...the ability to live on this planet in such a way that we don't destroy it," according to British economist Barbara Ward.

At an address given in the 1970's, Ward suggested that her listeners who "live in the world of privilege" remember the Jewish prophets, "all of whom were proponents of a moral sense of obligation to the poor and a judgment on the unmindful and uncaring rich."

Barbara Ward continued, "We will survive as a human community only if we can see the needs of others, and only if we keep power–including our own powerful desires–under some restraint and under some rule of law: the law of conscience and the law of community."

These points are still apt today. We have an obligation to assist the children of God who have little while we have so much.

As you have done, it shall be done to you. (Obadiah 15)

Our brothers and sisters are in need, Loving Father. Show us how to relieve their burdens of poverty and suffering.

Also Available

Have you enjoyed volume 41 of *Three Minutes a Day*? These other Christopher offerings may interest you:

- **News Notes** – published ten times a year on a variety of topics of current interest. One copy as published is free; quantity orders available.

- **Ecos Cristóforos** – Spanish translations of selected News Notes. Issued six times a year. One copy as published is free; quantity orders available.

- **Wall or Desk Appointment Calendar** – The Calendar offers an inspirational message for each day.

- **Videocassettes** – Christopher videos range from wholesome entertainment to serious discussions of family life and current social and spiritual issues.

For more information on The Christophers or to receive **News Notes, Ecos Cristóforos** or a catalogue:

The Christophers
12 East 48th Street
New York, NY 10017
Phone: 212-759-4050 / 888-298-4050
E-mail: mail@christophers.org
Website: www.christophers.org

The Christophers is a non-profit media organization founded in 1945. We share the message of personal responsibility and service to God and humanity with people of all faiths and no particular faith. Gifts are needed and tax-deductible. Our legal title for wills is The Christophers, Inc.